Guide to the Chattooga River

A Comprehensive Guide to the River
and Its Natural and Human History

Guide to the Chattooga River by Butch Clay

Copyright © 2012 by The Chattooga River Community and
   Conservation Fund
Printed in the United States of America
Published by Menasha Ridge Press
Distributed by Publishers Group West

This book was originally published by Chattooga River Publishing
   ISBN 0-9647083-0-2. Library of Congress catalog number 95-37215.

ISBN 978-0-89732-004-7

Cover design by Grant Tatum
Text design by Frank Logue
Cover photo donated by Beth Maynor. Beth is a freelance environ-
   mental photographer from Chelsea, Alabama.

Menasha Ridge Press
P.O. Box 43673
Birmingham, AL 35243
menasharidge.com

Publisher's Acknowledgments

As a publisher, it is rare to be given the space to thank those individuals
who make a project come to life. This book would not have come about
if it weren't for the extraordinary effort of numerous people; they all
deserve a "thank you." Dave Perrin developed the concept. The folks
at Menasha Ridge Press donated invaluable expertise and a significant
number of hours; Budd Zehmer managed the project; Grant Tatum
designed the cover; Beth Maynor donated the cover photograph; and
Frank Logue made a herculean effort in typesetting and map design.
A very special thanks to Southeastern Expeditions, Wildwater Limited,
and the Nantahala Outdoor Center for providng the financial backing
for this book. Finally, to all people on the River who made this book
possible.

Contents

Foreword 4

Introduction 6

Location and Topography 7

Physiography and Geology 9

Weather and Climate 11

Human History 12

Chattooga Plant Life 29

Chattooga Wildlife 34

Recreation on the Chattooga 41

Maps 50

Index 62

Foreword

The story of the Chattooga, or one version of the story, might go some
thing like this. A wild mountain river, born of the ineffably powerful
and patient forces of the earth's creative energy, ran on heedless and
unheeded to the sea for untold ages. Eventually people arrived, first Paleo-
Indians and later the Cherokee, each carving a small niche for their culture in this magnificent land each knowing this place in their own special
ways. Then, after having been mostly overlooked, avoided or ignored by
the mainstream of European settlers that swept over this so-called "empty"
continent like a plague of locusts, the river was, in a way, rediscovered. In
a rare moment of enlightened restraint, this river, and others of its kind,
were included among a small, select store of unspoiled wildlands, to be
set aside as a kind of "commons," a place reserved for the public good.

Thus, on May 10, 1974, the Chattooga became the first river east of
the Mississippi to be included in the National Wild and Scenic River System. The Chattooga garnered protection because it was, according to the
document recommending the river's unique qualities to Congress, a "clean,
free-flowing mountain stream located in a relatively undeveloped mountain setting...considered one of the finest white-water streams in the Southeast," and believed to be "an irreplaceable resource," whose best use was
as a "component of the National Wild and Scenic Rivers System." The
intervening twenty-odd years have only proven just how irreplaceable
the Chattooga is. Rivers this wild and beautiful are a long time in the
making, and we do not often have the opportunity to secure for ourselves
and our children such a fine remnant of an original America, which not so
very long ago was "wild and scenic" from shore to shore.

Still largely undisturbed by commercial or residential development,
the Chattooga is nevertheless not quite so wild and free as it was just
twenty years ago. Every year the Chattooga draws more and more people
to itself: tens of thousands come, to play or just to look, to escape urban
pressures and come into this incomparable river environment. More boat-
ers, more rafters, more anglers, more hikers and campers: Our need for
untrammeled space where we can recreate and renew ourselves grows
and grows, but the space to do it in grows only more dear. And so even as
we put greater and greater pressure on the river, our admiration becomes
necessarily more protective, our need to know and understand the river
resource more critical. The Chattooga environment has, in fact, become

so valuable that we find ourselves now in a most ironic and unenviable position: We just might be loving the place to death.

Aldo Leopold once wrote: "Recreational development is a job not of building roads into lovely country, but of building receptivity into the still unlovely human mind." Leopold did not care much for public recreation as it was usually practiced in his day. Recreation, he believed, could become as dangerous to the health of our intact wild places as any other extractive use such as logging or mining. But Leopold knew that in order for us as a people to protect and enhance the only wild lands we had remaining, we would need nothing short of an almost total redirection of American values.

This is where the Wild and Scenic Rivers Act in general (which has its roots in the wilderness movement) and the Chattooga in particular, offer us such invaluable prospects. What we need is more than a park or a playground. What we need is precisely what the Chattooga is so uniquely endowed to provide–a place where the protection of nature's diversity and the study of nature's web of inter-connected life forms and processes take precedence over human uses and demands.

Not that the human aspect should be totally ignored, for like any of our surviving wildlands, the Chattooga provides us with a remnant of the primitive landscape out of which America was forged. In this respect the river is an important cultural resource, illustrating how our nation has taken to its current place of residence on this continent. We set aside the Chattooga in recognition of the important part wilderness played in making our culture, and in doing so, we recognize, finally, that we need wilderness to survive as a culture.

The Chattooga, it appears, is destined to be become to an even greater extent what it already is–an island of naturalness surrounded by encroaching dangers that would compromise the integrity of the river environment. The beginning of real protection for this river and places like it is to be found, ultimately, in the sort of understanding of the natural world that this book hopefully in its own meager fashion engenders.

About This Book

The Chattooga Sourcebook is designed to be opened anywhere and read without needing to know what goes before or after. However, if readers were to go from beginning to end, they would learn about the topography and geology of the river, to give them an idea how the Chattooga fits into the scheme of things, how it came about and how it interlocks with regional ecosystems. The book then goes on to look at human history, from the pre-historic to contemporary times. Nature is examined next, looking at some of the flora and fauna that may be found here. Finally, the sourcebook turns to recreation, noting some of the activities readers can experience in order to enjoy the Chattooga River more fully. At the end of the book is a map of the river as well as the major trails and trail heads. Illustrations and photographs help to round off the picture.

Introduction

The Chattooga River begins as springs and rivulets high on the impressive southern flank of Whiteside mountain, near Cashiers, North Carolina, at the crest of the eastern continental divide, and flows roughly fifty miles to the upper Piedmont, forming the boundary between Georgia and South Carolina for much of its length. In its descent, the Chattooga pours over rocky ledges and plunges down steep, gorge-bound rapids, first falling precipitously, then slowing and gathering itself in quiet pools beneath hemlock, laurel and rhododendron until it falls again–in the classic fashion of a mountain river–alternately whispering and thundering its way toward the sea. Even though it lies comparatively close to major urban areas, the river environment retains an unspoiled, primitive character that is unsurpassed in the Southeastern states. It is one of the East's longest and largest free-flowing mountain rivers still relatively unaltered by human hands, flowing through unbroken forests, usually out of sight of farms, fields, houses, roads or any other signs of commercial, agricultural or residential development.

One of the premiere paddling rivers in the country, the Chattooga is by now synonymous with challenging whitewater and is heavily used by both private and commercial floaters, who come to run its demanding rapids and revel in its refreshing wildness. Equally renowned for its trout fishing, the Chattooga is a major destination for anglers in the Southeast. Not least, the corridor's sixty miles of foot trails and otherwise outstanding natural scenery make the river a favored retreat for hikers and campers as well. Since roads are limited—only four bridges span the river in roughly forty-five miles of continuous National Forest ownership on the main branch—it is an ideal place for hunters, floaters, campers, hikers and anglers to leave their cars and their cares behind and experience the solitude and the sanctity of one of the last best places left in the East.

After its designation by Congress as a Wild and Scenic River in 1974, a corridor was created out of lands immediately adjacent to the river in the Nantahala, Sumter and Chattahoochee National Forests, in North and South Carolina, and Georgia, respectively. All roads within the quarter-mile corridor were closed (with the exception of major roads already in place and two roads, one going to Sandy Ford, the other a serious four-wheel drive to Earls Ford). Parking lots and put-in trails were constructed, a permit system was implemented to facilitate the monitoring of river use, and regulations were enacted in efforts toward visitor safety. The Wild and Scenic corridor is currently comprised of some 15,432 acres and extends on average quarter-mile on either side of the river. The corridor protects only the land adjacent to the main river and the West Fork—not the tributaries or sections of the river that flow through private land. The entire Chattooga watershed, in fact, totals some 180,795 acres, or roughly 278 square miles.

Location and Topography

The Southeastern Blue Ridge Escarpment, an abrupt, cliff-like land form, forms the boundary between the high mountains of the Blue Ridge and the more gentle, rolling hills of the Piedmont. Characterized by a 28-mile-wide, ten-mile long, south-facing embayment, the escarpment is dissected by the Chattooga, Eastatoe, Toxaway, Horsepasture, Thompson and Whitewater Rivers, all of which cut through deep, beautiful gorges on their two thousand foot descent to the upper Piedmont. The region is truly rugged and mountainous, with high, narrow ridge tops rising above deeply incised, almost V-shaped river valleys and gorges. The ancient weathered face of the region gives eloquent testimony to the patient power of water.

The Chattooga is generally not as steep in gradient as the other rivers of the escarpment, for it does not cut directly across the escarpment as do most of its sister rivers. For most of its length, the Chattooga tends southwestwardly along a ridge of mountains known as the Chattooga escarpment or Chattooga Ridge. This ridge, rising nine hundred feet above the river in places, divides the Chattooga watershed from the upper Piedmont. The river cuts through the steepest portion of the gorge in its first twenty miles, dropping on average 84 feet per mile. Thereafter, the river gorge is generally wider with more gentle mountains on either side, the average gradient only 22 feet per mile. Only after descending to one thou-

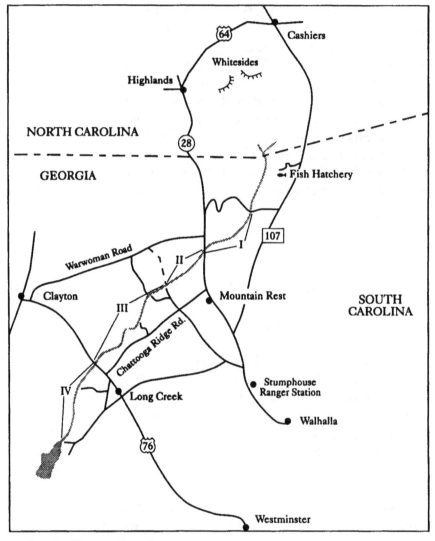

Guide to the Chattooga River–8

sand feet in elevation does the Chattooga turn back to the southeast and escape the escarpment near Lake Tugaloo, the highest lake on the main branch of the Savannah.

Though the Chattooga by itself is unique enough, the river watershed is actually but part of a larger whole, the Southern Appalachian ecosystem, which spans six national forests altogether. The mountains that form the backbone of this ecosystem extend from extreme northwest South Carolina and northern Georgia northward through western North Carolina and eastern Tennessee into southern Virginia, towering over the plains of the Cumberland Plateau to the west and the Piedmont to the east. Thus the Chattooga Wild and Scenic River, like the Great Smoky Mountains and the Blue Ridge Parkway, is an integral part of the largest assemblage of public lands east of the Mississippi, an area comprising some 3.7 million acres.

Physiography and Geology

Much of the wild natural character of the Chattooga gorge is ultimately the product of geological forces. Hence, the story of the green, living river environment must begin with rock, for geology is the cornerstone upon which all other understanding of natural history rests.

The Blue Ridge mountains in which the Chattooga originates are among the world's oldest, ancient even by geological standards. Most of the Blue Ridge consists of Precambrian formations deposited before the advent of vertebrate life. The rock of the Chattooga drainage is mostly composed of meta-sediments—sandstones and shales—laid down approximately 600 to 750 million years ago. The mountains themselves were the product of continental collision over 350 million years ago. According to some geologists, portions of the Blue Ridge may have been higher originally than the Rockies—as high, some say, as the present-day Himalayas. Repeated periods of uplift and erosion were the forces behind this landscape as we know it.

Once the mountains were uplifted, water became the primary natural agent at work on the land. Though the rock of these mountains was very erosion-resistant—a fact which helps explain the deep narrow valleys and steep slopes of the region—the inexorable forces of weather and water wore away at the jagged peaks through millennia, lowering and rounding them. A warm climate, persistent rains, and the microscopically efficient force of constant biologic activity all combined to enhance the erosive effects of millions of years of exposure.

Today, the mountains of the Blue Ridge are considered to be "subdued," meaning they have lost so much of their original height and steepness that they are now only a mantle of decayed rock overlying much older Precambrian bedrock.

Geologists tell us that the Chattooga may have undergone at least one major change in flow direction. Until relatively recent times, in geological terms, the Chattooga flowed not into the Savannah but continued on southwesterly into the Chattahoochee riverbed and then on to the Gulf of Mexico. Through the process of "stream capture," the Savannah River gradually ate back at its northern headland until it intersected the river channel to the north, probably somewhere near the present day location of Lake Yonah, thereby diverting the Chattooga to the Atlantic.

Ineffably ancient as the geologic history of the area may be, geologic process in the Chattooga gorge is not confined to the past; it continues to this day, though usually the change is slow enough to escape our detection. As weathering proceeds, portions of the ridges sometimes give way and fall into the ravines below them, often taking the forest with them. Many of the rocks in the Chattooga riverbed probably arrived in such fashion. However, these boulders and rocks do not remain stationary. During extended downpours or deluges, violent floodwaters can rampage down the slopes of the gorge, tearing away rocks, uprooting trees and dislodging tons of debris, which then washes down into the river. Millennial floods–great deluges thought to occur once in a thousand years–may make drastic changes in the rivercourse overnight.

As noted above, the rock of the Chattooga gorge is metamorphic, and consists predominantly of crystalline schists (a comparatively soft rock composed primarily of laminated mica flakes) and gneiss (a harder rock with characteristic dark and light bands). Minerals present are commonly of three types: *muscovite*, which shows itself as sparkling flakes of mica in the river sands; *amphibole*, which is a dark, iron-rich mineral that oxidizes and lends the local soils their characteristic red color; and *white quartz* and *feldspar*, often apparent in distinctive veins intruded into other granitic rock. Rarer minerals present are *garnets*, which appear as small, glassy, red grains, and *soapstone* or *steatite*, a white-to-green talc, easily carvable and used by early native inhabitants in the area make bowls and pipes.

Weather and Climate

The rich natural diversity of the Chattooga gorge results from a number of factors, including its elevation, its latitude, and its proximity to the mountains. Climate, also, has a major affect upon the river environment, including precipitation, temperature, prevailing wind direction and the amount of sunshine received.

Generally, in the summer, the weather in the Chattooga area is much cooler and more pleasant than Piedmont areas not very far away, which can remain hot and humid for extended periods. Weather conditions from May to September are often ideal for float trips, extended hikes, fishing and overnight camping along the river. Rain showers can be frequent in early summer but seldom is anything more than light camping gear required for overnight stays. Daytime temperatures earlier in the season, from March through April, and later, from October through November, are usually suitable for fishing, hiking, and hunting, though cold water temperatures and chilly nights may limit extended float trips and overnight camping.

The average annual air temperature for the entire river is 60. The temperature reaches 90, on average, 24 days a year, and plunges to freezing or below about 74 days each year. The mountain slopes to the north can get up to 50 inches of snow a year, while the river itself averages only about 3.5 inches; snow seldom lingers in either place. Winds from the southwest prevail for roughly ten months of the year and from the northeast during September and October. Average wind speed is 8 1/2 mph.

There is considerable seasonal variation in the amount of rainfall in the Chattooga country. October and November are usually the driest months, often a time of "Indian Summer." Rainfall gradually increases into March, peaks, then moderates into June. Late June can bring a wet period that lasts until early September, during which time thunderstorms can be frequent.

In general, the topography of the Chattooga river watershed may be divided into two "climate belts" or "thermal zones." The climate of the northern half is affected by the higher elevations—with cold winters and mild summers. The average temperature is 39 in January, 70 in July. Rainfall in the northern section is evenly distributed throughout the year, usually exceeding 80 inches annually. Except for the Pacific Northwest, the Chattooga headwaters are, in fact, the only area of the coterminous U.S. that receives more than 80 inches a year. The southern half of the river has a climate of the humid continental type. Winters are cool, summers relatively hot. The average temperature for the southern end of the river is 42 in January, and 77 in July. Rainfall in the southern reaches of the river averages 60 inches a year.

It's worth noting that the former inhabitants of these mountains, the Cherokee, divided the year into just two basic periods: "gogi," the warm time from April to October, when they lived outside both night and day, and "gola," the cold time in between. This beguiling simplicity belies the fact that they were constant, careful observers of seasonal variations in the surrounding mountain lands. The month of May they might refer to as "when turkey cocks gobble," June as "strawberry time" and late fall, when hickory nuts and acorns littered the forest floor, as the "time of rutting bucks."

Human History

The rich Chattooga valley, like all of the Southern Appalachians, was not "discovered" by Europeans. Long before any Caucasians appeared here, the first Americans followed creeks and rivers and game trails up into these hills to occupy a fertile, temperate mountain country whose aboriginal lineaments we can only try to imagine. Native Americans lived here for thousands of years before pale-faced men from distant lands began pushing into the continent from the coasts in an inexorable human tide that would decimate much of the indigenous human and animal populations and radically alter the face of the continent.

The first humans to come into the Chattooga country were probably bands of Paleo-Indians who likely followed animal trails down through Rabun Gap or came up from coastal lowlands to this region twelve thousand or so years ago. As hunter-gatherers, these native peoples likely lived in camps, moving from time to time as they followed the herds of deer and elk and foraged for hickory nuts, chinkapins, chestnuts and other wild plant foods. Their material possessions were probably limited to those they could carry on their backs: axes, knives, scrapers, bows, arrows and bowls. Their sole sustenance was the native ecosystem, then a teeming hunting ground that had itself existed untouched for thousands upon thousands of years. Likely these early peoples knew the Chattooga country in all its dense and jumbled detail far better than any modern human ever has.

We have no direct evidence of Paleo-Indian presence in Chattooga watershed though much evidence elsewhere confirms an early Native American presence in the general area. Throughout the southeast, archeologists have found artifacts dating to the Archaic period—between 8000 and 1000 B.C.—when descendants of the Paleo-Indians lived. What evidence of human occupation that has been found in this area (prior to that of the Cherokee Indians) includes thousand year old Etowah artifacts as well as even older Connestee artifacts dating to around the third or fourth century A.D.

The Cherokee

Though the Cherokee were certainly not the first native peoples ever to occupy the Chattooga country, they were its proud possessors when Europeans first appeared on the scene. Even before it became the frontier between the mountain-loving Cherokee and the land-hungry English on the coast, the Chattooga likely represented the boundary between the Cherokee and their war-like neighbors to the south, the Creeks.

A summary look at their reconstructed history tells us that the Cherokee were once numbered among the powerful Great Lakes Iroquoian family of Indians. At some point, however, the Cherokee began a slow migration southward and settled in the southeast, either eradicating or displacing the tribes that lay in their path. We do not know exactly how long they had occupied the mountains before their first contact with Europeans, but by the time significant contact with the English ensued in the seventeenth century, the Cherokee had established themselves along the great mountain barrier dividing the English settlements on the east coast from the French or Spanish along the Mississippi and the Ohio.

The name "Cherokee" has no meaning in the tribe's native language and probably derived from sources outside the Cherokee nation. They called themselves the "Ani Yunwiya," the "principle, or real people." The Cherokee were in essence Native American mountaineers, holding at their cultural peak an area of about 40,000 square miles comprised of mostly mountainous land that would become parts of Virginia, Tennessee, Georgia, Alabama, Kentucky and the Carolinas. Their principal towns lay along the headwaters of the Savannah, the Hiawassee, the Tuckasegee and along the length of the Little Tennessee to its confluence with the Tennessee. The Chattooga area must surely have been important to them, if we are to judge by the fact that in 1715 their nation's eastern center and most sacred town was at Tugaloo, not many miles downstream from the confluence of the Chattooga and the Tallulah rivers.

While they flourished, the Cherokee hunted and foraged in the hills and farmed the rich valley soils near their riverside settlements. Corn, beans and squash, the "three sisters," were their principle crops. They were great lovers of sport and played a ball game with martial fervor in nearby fields reserved for such pursuits. And though exceedingly warlike, they were, like most Native Americans, a profoundly spiritual people with highly developed ceremonial observances intended to ensure their continued fidelity to the Immortals of the mountains and the waters.

Much of this spirituality and culture would have been lost if not for the efforts of the ethnographer, James Mooney. Mooney lamented the fact that the Cherokee, like many other Carolina tribes, had been reduced almost to extinction by war, pestilence, slaving and, not least, whiskey, before anyone ever thought to inquire into just who they were, how they lived and what they believed. He had the prescience to gather much invaluable information from the Cherokee about their land, history and beliefs in the last years of the nineteenth century, just as such priceless lore was disappearing.

Mooney noted the Cherokee's tendency to attach a story or a legend to any prominent rock or bend in the river in the "Old Cherokee country." And it's worth noting that the Cherokee thought that the streams and springs of the mountains, if followed back far enough, would lead to the underworld of spirit beings. They told tales of "water cougars" and "spearfinger ogres" who haunted the deep mountain fastnesses. The sound of the falls and rapids of their mountain rivers they referred to as the voice of "Long Man," the river god, who spoke a language that spiritual people could understand. As a people almost obsessively concerned with the purity and the health of the human spirit, one of their most important observances was the "going to water" rite, a ceremonial immersion in the river believed to purify and make clean the living soul.

As with most peoples, the Cherokee had their own creation myth. They believed the great mountains that spanned their domain, the "Blue Wall" or the "Great Blue Hills of God" as they termed them, had been formed when the original sky beings overpopulated their land in the heavens and turned their eyes toward the earth, which at the time was nothing but water. The sky beings—people and animals—sent down a water beetle in search of land, who promptly began diving to the great ocean's bottom to bring up mud; this mud grew and grew until it became the lands of earth. Since the earth was still soft and muddy, the great grandfather buzzard flew down to dry the wet earth by beating his wings down low over the land. By the time this mythic bird reached the Cherokee lands, he had grown very tired. Flying low to the ground, the great wing beats made impressions upon the soft earth, forming the hills and hollows of the Cherokee land.

Cherokee Settlements and Chattooga Town

Not far from where Highway 28 crosses the river today lies the remains of a small Cherokee village called Chattooga town. Much of our knowledge about this town and the Cherokee society has been expanded and enriched through a six year study of this area, headed by the University of Tennessee archaeologist, Dr. Gerald Schroedl.

In the Cherokee mountain homeland, there were few flood plains large enough to support large population centers as were common in other parts of the Southeast. The Cherokee tended to cluster in smaller settlements near rivers and streams where the land was level and fertile and sources of fish and game were abundant. These settlements usually consisted of a few family dwellings constructed of clay and thatch and some accompanying small ceremonial structures nearby. Chattooga Town was one such settlement.

Chattooga Town was a Lower Town, one of a number of Cherokee villages on the headwaters of the Savannah that comprised the eastern branch of the Cherokee, one of three settlement enclaves of a widely dispersed nation that also included the Middle Towns in western North Carolina and the Overhills in eastern Tennessee.

Careful study at Chattooga Town has revealed the sites of various domestic structures that suggest a village of no more than ten to fifteen widely scattered dwellings and a population just under a hundred souls. Moreover, excavation has also revealed the remains of a townhouse or council house; unearthing this important ceremonial structure constitutes a major find for archeologists—no other Lower Town council house has ever been investigated. The center of all important political and ceremonial occasions, this circular structure was about forty-five to fifty feet in diameter and made of wattle and daubing; it was supported by eight central posts and was most likely covered with bark shingles or a thatched roof. Evidence suggests this structure had been rebuilt at least once, the later townhouse constructed directly over the earlier site.

According to Dr. Schroedl, the last townhouse apparently burned down about 1735. Items discovered here, especially those of European origin such as kaolin pipestems and glass trade beads, are valuable in helping archeologists understand important aspects of Cherokee social and ceremonial activities. These artifacts also help understand the European influence on the Cherokee culture as the Europeans began to exert their presence in the Carolina backcountry. It was in fact unusual for a town of this size and remoteness to have a townhouse; that it did have such a structure probably owes to the town's relative isolation—it was seven miles over rugged mountain terrain to the next Cherokee village—as to its location on one of the primary trails to the Middle Towns over the mountains.

It appears that by the 1740s or 1750s, Chattooga Town had ceased to function as a townsite, which might reflect the degenerated state of Cherokee/British relations, particularly after 1758. The town's abandonment also reflects the scourge of smallpox that swept inland after its introduction into the Carolinas by a slave ship around the year 1738. Though it apparently ceased to exist as a functioning village, Chattooga Town could have retained individual households as late as 1816, the date the Cherokee formally relinquished control of their last holdings in South Carolina. This loss unfortunately only presaged others, which would culminate in the cruel Cherokee Removal Act of 1838, effectively eliminating the Cherokee from their ancestral mountain homeland.

The First Contact—De Soto

Recorded history in the Chattooga country begins in 1540 with Hernando De Soto, who with his ruffian band of six hundred men and two hundred horses, drove hogs, bloodhounds and captive Native American bearers up the Savannah looking for gold and empire, offering in return only enslavement and disease to the Cherokees. While on the lower Savannah at a Native American town named Cofitachiqui, De Soto found hatchets and other copper items that seemed to be mixed with gold. Steered by the natives northward into the mountainous interior in pursuit of mines, the Spanish came to "a province called Chalaque"—a Cherokee territory probably somewhere on the headwaters of the Keowee river. One chronicler wrote that the way was very rough, with "lofty ridges drenched with continual rain, the rivers always rising and narrowing the land." The Spanish described this land as the poorest they had seen for corn and observed that the inhabitants lived on wild roots, herbs and on the game they took with bows and arrows.

De Soto continued north a time until he turned to the west and crossed a high range, undoubtedly the Blue Ridge. The streams on the other side flowed in the opposite direction—leading to the Mississippi. There is some question as to just where De Soto crossed the Blue Ridge. Local tradition has it that De Soto ascended the Winding Stairs Trail and crossed the Chattooga around Burrel's Ford, while some historians believe he crossed the mountains farther to the north. Howsoever, De Soto made it to the Mississippi, where he died of malaria.

The English

After the Spanish there came a hundred years or so of peace for the Cherokee, their last respite before the English began pouring into their country. Though the Virginia English had made contact with the Cherokee by 1654, significant contact between the Cherokee and the English of South Carolina did not begin until sometime after the first colony was established at Charles Towne in 1670. At first, the rugged, deep forests of the high Blue Ridge mountains formed a barrier to hold in check the settlers, but by the later years of the seventeenth century, English Carolinians were already probing deeper and deeper into the mysterious country to the west, carrying English influence and enterprise beyond the Appalachians and into the valleys of the Tennessee and Mississippi Rivers.

The first advances into Cherokee land came by river and land routes that followed Indian trading paths. The main trade route, the Cherokee Path, wandered along the west bank of the Saluda River north past the Congaree, near present-day Columbia. It continued to the northwest, proceeding first to the outpost of "Ninety-Six" and then on to Keowee and other Cherokee towns lying at the head of the Savannah. This trail eventually passed through Chattooga Town and on over the mountains to the western Cherokee towns.

The Carolina trade was built upon deerskins, which were in demand for the manufacture of military uniforms for the troops of European armies. South Carolina export figures suggest the magnitude of this trade; by the early 1700s, exports had already exceeded 50,000 hides annually. The traders offered the Cherokee a variety of items as compensation: firearms, ammunition, iron axes, knives, hoes, glass trade beads, mirrors, clothing, and, unfortunately, rum, despite its early prohibition.

Relations between the English and Cherokee were oftentimes remarkably amicable, although these relations became strained and degenerated into war in 1760. These early misfortunes were only the first of many to come. The Cherokee, having dutifully sided with the British in the French and Indian conflicts, made the mistake in the American Revolution of taking the English side again. This loyalty to the Crown eventually forced the Cherokee into more treaties and land cessions.

Settlement, Frontier Outposts and Land Grants

By the 1780s, the Cherokee were a different people from the powerful nation that had negotiated with the English just fifty years earlier. Devastated by war and disease, constricted in their ever-shrinking hunting grounds and disenchanted with the boundless greed of the Americans, the Cherokee had few places to go. After the 1780s, they were driven ever westward and southwestward into north Georgia, the former territory of the Creeks.

Inevitably, settlers began to move into land once occupied by the Cherokee. According to the Chattooga Wild and Scenic River Proposal document, it was the quest for gold in the 1700s that first brought white men into this area. One early gold mine was located on Ammons Branch, two miles from the Chattooga. It yielded little gold, and gold mining soon declined. The settlers that remained turned to agriculture and located their farms and villages away from the river, back between the main mountain ranges.

Shortly after the War of Independence, a group led by Colonel Benjamin Cleveland received land grants from Georgia to settle along the Tugaloo River. These were the first known "domestic white settlers" of present-day Oconee county. When this land was ceded to South Carolina in 1787 by the Treaty of Beaufort, the state re-granted these lands on the east side of Tugaloo to these settlers.

Throughout the 1780s, "Indian troubles" continued intermittently, and by 1792 the situation with the Creeks and bands of dissident Cherokee was tense enough to warrant the construction of several small blockhouse outposts along the South Carolina frontier. A guard post was built near the Tugaloo River during the Revolution, Norwood's Station, which served as a frontier strong point. Oconee Station was another backcountry outpost. These outposts guarded a frontier country that ran some forty miles to the north and east of the Tugaloo river.

In addition to protecting white settlers, these frontier stations also helped forestall white encroachments upon Native American lands to the west. The Governor of South Carolina thought the stations necessary to protect the whites "against the inroads of the Indians," and, likewise, to protect Native Americans from certain "designing and evil disposed persons" such as could be found in plenty in the Carolina backcountry at the time. Oconee Station appears to have been the only military outpost in operation after 1796; by 1799 the frontier was pacified enough for Oconee Station to cease military functions and served only as an Indian trading post.

Early Naturalists in the Area—
William Bartram and Andre Michaux

One early exception to the usual predatory frontier type that roamed the backwoods of Appalachia was William Bartram a native of Philadelphia and a good friend to Benjamin Franklin. This noted botanist, artist, traveler, and writer, made his way—usually alone and on horseback—through much of Florida, Georgia and the Carolinas in the years just before the American Revolution. William first visited the southern wilds of Florida and coastal Georgia while on expedition with his father. The experience apparently had a major formative effect upon William's naturalist's instincts, if we are to judge by the trained, close-observing naturalist's eye he cast upon the territories he wandered through from 1773 until 1778.

Bartram's book about his travels and discoveries, *Travels Of William Bartram*, published in 1791, actually recounts his crossing of the Chattooga and of the high mountains between the headwaters of the Savannah and the Tennessee Rivers. It was during this crossing that Bartram discovered the Fraser Magnolia, which he found in the Chattooga watershed not far from Rabun Bald. Elsewhere in the book Bartram extols the "sublime forests" that he found throughout the southern mountains. He writes about black oaks thirty feet around, beeches and sweet gums one hundred and fifty feet tall, and chestnut trees thirteen feet thick at the base. Today his book is referred to for valuable hints about the nature of the native Chattooga river ecosystem, as scientist and environmentalists try to piece together what the watershed was like before the catastrophic alterations of the historical period.

Another great plant hunter, the French botanist Andre Michaux, explored the southern mountains—and crossed the Chattooga—while on commission to search the New World for botanical curiosities to take back to the French Royal Court. Michaux crossed the Chattooga in 1787, near Ellicott's Rock, searching for the mountain magnolia that Bartram had described twelve years earlier. Michaux's journal gives hint of the effect that the steep mountain paths and deep, thickly tangled forests had upon him. The deep ravines overhung by high peaks and choked with dense growth through which he struggled dismayed him; he fretted about rattlesnakes and the inability of his "savage" guides to produce any game. Corn meal washed down with creek water became his daily fare, while the noise and spray of so many waterfalls and the torrential rains that went on unceasingly for days discouraged and confused him.

When his young frontiersman guide, who had himself spent five months among the Native Americans and could understand their speech, voiced his suspicion that the Indian guides were themselves lost and clueless as to how to reach the Tennessee, Michaux, low on food and dispirited, decided to turn back to the frontier settlement of Seneca. Michaux later came close to the Chattooga again when he returned to the escarpment gorge country and discovered near the junction of the Horsepasture and Toxaway rivers (now buried underneath the waters of Lake Jocassee) the rare spring flower that would eventually be called Oconee Bells.

Ellicott Rock

When King George II issued the Georgia Crown Charter in 1732, the northern boundary betweeb Georgia and North Carolina was set at the 35th parallel. However neither Georgia nor North Carolina could agree exactly where the north-to-south dividing line was. The disputed strip became a refuge for outlaws and other shady characters and was known as the "Orphan Strip." In 1811, Georgia's Governor Mitchell contracted Andrew Ellicott, a renowned surveyor from Pennsylvania, to survey and mark the boundary between the two states. This Ellicott did by inscribing on the boundary marker rock "NC-GA." Then, in 1813, South and North Carolina decided that their shared border needed clearer demarcation, so commissioners were appointed to establish that state line. The original Ellicott's Rock could not be found, so the surveyors found and marked another rock, roughly 500 feet down river, with the letters "Lat 35/AD

1813tNC+SC." This rock is now known as the "Commissioner's Rock." In 1966, a 3,584 acre National Forest Scenic Area was established to protect the historic site and environment, and in 1973 Ellicott's Rock was listed in the National Register of Historic Places.

Early Settlement and Development—1700s and 1800s

Local tradition has it that the lands immediately adjacent to the Chattooga river, which had first been only hunting grounds to the widely dispersed Cherokee, were not occupied in early settler times. Mill's map of 1830 seems to bear this out, showing instead more settlement activity on the nearby Chauga River.

According to the Chattooga Wild and Scenic River Proposal document, the earliest known settlement in the Chattooga Gorge occurred in

1830, near the Monroe House, where about fifty acres of land were cleared. Other early settler activity later scattered around Burrel's Ford and around the present day location of Highway 28 bridge.

The steep mountain country through which the Chattooga flows severely limited the development of the area and had a profound isolating effect upon the people who settled there. Thus the settler history of the Chattooga country was quintessentially that of most of Appalachia: For a very long time the mainstream simply bypassed the mountaineers, who like the Native Americans before them (or, for that matter, any other life form taking refuge in these mountains) had isolated themselves in the bottoms and the coves between the high ridges. Living a life of subsistence, these settlers got by any way they could.

The early white settlers were principally Scotch-Irish who had emigrated from the north of Ireland. They cleared small farmsteads in the coves and "hollers" wherever level land and crude tools of wood and hand-forged scrap metal allowed, employing the natural forest materials at hand for cabins and fences and letting their cattle and hogs range free in the rich surrounding woods. Wild turkey, squirrel, deer, bear and rabbit complemented their vegetable diets of cane and corn and other grains. Corn became their staple, and eventually their primary cash crop, as it was mashed, fermented and distilled into whiskey. Though their generally poor farming practices and the highly erodable soils of the area combined to waste a lot of resources in some areas, leading to an inevitable decline in standard of living, all in all the impact of these pioneer folk on the vast expanse of primeval Appalachian forest was minimal. For over a century, the mountain settlers were left alone or otherwise overlooked by the great industrial developers who avoided the rough, hardscrabble Appalachian mountains and pursued instead the more easily exploitable riches of the Midwest and Far West.

The Blue Ridge Railroad

This railroad, also called the Black Diamond Railroad, was designed to connect Charleston, South Carolina, with Cincinnati by way of North Carolina and Tennessee. Chartered in 1852, the rail line was to run via Abbeville, Anderson and Walhalla, South Carolina through Rabun Gap and down the Little Tennessee to Knoxville. A series of companies contracted to build the line, which at the time was expected to require three big bridges, many huge fills and cuts, and twelve tunnels, three of which to be built in South Carolina. All failed.

From 1853 to 1859, the state of South Carolina sank more than a million dollars in the one-and-a-half-mile Stumphouse Tunnel, which fell behind schedule due to the unyielding nature of the blue granite rock. The railroad reached West Union, and three-fourths of the grade work from there to Stumphouse had been completed when Fort Sumter was bombarded in Charleston Harbor, effectively terminating the endeavor. Had it been completed, Charleston would have become the major East Coast deep water shipping port, and the history of the Chattooga area might have developed quite differently. Today, remains of the Stumphouse Tunnel can be found just north of Walhalla along Highway 28.

Later Settlement and Development

By the late 1800s and the early 1900s, life in the mountains began to change. As the more easily accessed forests of the North and Midwest were exhausted and new technologies were developed, Northern timbermen began to pursue the beautiful and dense hardwood forests of the southern mountains. Soon timber barons bought up mountain land here, as they did throughout the Appalachians. (This author was told by Mr. Oliver Ridley, now deceased, that he could remember his grandfather selling the big trees on their farmstead on the banks of the Chattooga for 25 cents each.) The "cut-out and get-out" era that followed brought a brief boom of prosperity to some mountain areas, especially those the logging rails could reach.

Like many other richly forested Appalachian river basins, most of the Chattooga drainage was cut over with no provision for reforestation. Logs had to be floated downstream to mill. Loggers often employed splash dams, which were crude log dams designed to impound water where cut logs might be pooled—the idea being to "let go" the dam and transport the timber downstream on the rushing outflow. Another method was the pile dam. With the aid of draft animals, big logs were jammed against trees that overhung the water, thereby creating a crude damn that was dynamited at the appropriate time—usually when floodwaters promised a quick, sure trip downstream to the mill.

The catastrophic effect of these logging methods upon river and streamside areas is easily imagined. Also, the slash and debris left to lie in large outlying areas of cut over forests soon turned to tinder, which resulted in huge uncontrolled fires that burned away the protective humus-cover of the forest floor in many watersheds. Soon thereafter, with nothing to hold in place the soils of steep, denuded slopes, the naturally high rainfall of the mountains brought rampaging floods which further scoured and degraded the forest land. The Weeks Law of 1911 authorized the Forest Service to begin buying up these ravaged, cut over and abandoned "lands that nobody wanted" for the protection of watersheds. Much of the land now in the three national forests surrounding the Chattooga was acquired in this way. Forest Service reforestation and erosion and fire control measures helped restore the wasted farms and hillsides to forests.

As the twentieth century progressed, most major transportation routes and settlement continued to by-pass the Chattooga to the west, north, and

Poor forestry practices took their toll on the Chattooga drainage, until the Weeks Law of 1911 authorized the Forest Service to begin buying up ravaged lands for the protection of the watershed.

east. Farm employment in the area was briefly invigorated in the 1930s by poultry production, but soon large feed companies made it impossible for the small farmer to compete. As farming declined, large numbers of people left the rural areas nearby and sought jobs in the cities. Though the depressed conditions in the mountains made for a hardscrabble existence for many a hard working mountain family, the remoteness and uncertain living conditions served to shield the area from some of the more undesirable effects of modern urbanization and sprawl.

The Civilian Conservation Corps

On March 4, 1933, a few days after assuming the Office of the Presidency, Franklin D. Roosevelt announced plans for the creation of a "conservation army." The creation of the Civilian Conservation Corps was designed to help cope with the severe economic crisis facing the nation. At first, the CCC was seen as a forestry organization for fire-fighting, tree planting and flood control. However, it was soon realized that the Corps

This photograph of the confluence of the Chattooga and Tugaloo Rivers shows the rivers during logging's heyday.

might be put to work toward the construction of forest improvement—building roads, trails, buildings and recreation sites. Just in the area around the Chattooga, the CCC accomplished an impressive list of projects. They built Oconee State Park, the Walhalla Fish Hatchery, Stumphouse Ranger Station, the Chattooga and Yellow Branch picnic Areas, and the Long Mountain Fire Tower. They also rebuilt Highway 107, Cassidy Bridge Road and Whetstone Road, and a significant portion of Chattooga Ridge Road. Much of this work was done by hand—clearing the land, mining and hauling the necessary rock. Other tasks the CCC accomplished are not so obvious now but were most vital at the time, not the least of which was the erosion control work done on the often worn-out farms that the Forest Service had newly purchased.

The Chattooga and the Wild and Scenic River System

After 1960, people in the United States began to wake up to the ravages of decades of mindless misuse and abuse of their natural environment; years of dam-building and river channelization projects had made wild, free-flowing rivers increasingly rare. People began to realize how little truly wild land remained. This environmental awakening culminated, after long struggle, in the passage of the National Wilderness Protection Act of 1964. Nevertheless, some people, apparently alarmed at the intensity of debate over our last wildlands, felt that more needed to be done to safeguard our last unspoiled rivers.

At the urging of conservationists and upon the recommendation of then Secretary of the Interior Stuart Udall, the Department of Agriculture in 1964 identified 650 still-wild rivers or parts of rivers that seemed to merit further study. This list was eventually reduced to twenty-two rivers for detailed field study. In October of 1968, the Wild and Scenic Rivers Act became law, and began with these words:

> It is hereby declared to be the policy of the United States that certain selected rivers of the Nation which, with their immediate environments, possess outstandingly remarkable scenic, recreational, geologic, fish and wildlife, historic, cultural, or other similar values, shall be preserved in free-flowing condition, and that they and their immediate environments shall be protected for the benefit and enjoyment of present and future generations

Initially, only eight rivers were protected: the Rio Grande in New Mexico, the St. Croix in Minnesota and in Wisconsin, the Wolf in Wisconsin, The Eleven Point in Missouri, California's Middle Fork of the Feather, and in Idaho both the Middle Fork of the Clearwater and the Middle Fork of the Salmon. Unlike many of the eastern rivers, most of these rivers were already on Federal lands, none of them were deemed of national importance, and perhaps most important, none of them were slated for Federal hydroelectric development. Twenty-seven other potentially more controversial rivers were named to be studied for possible inclusion in the wild river system. In the Southeastern States, only three other rivers besides the Chattooga were initially designated for study: the Suwannee in Georgia, the Obed in central Tennessee and the Buffalo in Arkansas. The Chattooga was the only southern Appalachian river proposed.

Study of the Chattooga began in 1969 with the assignment of a Forest

Service field team to gather and analyze data on the river and its environment. This study eventually resulted in a document by the Department of Agriculture recommending the Chattooga River to the National Wild and Scenic Rivers System.

As part of the Chattooga River study, two public meetings were held: The first, in Highlands, North Carolina, in December 1969, and the second in Clayton, Georgia, in March of 1970. After each of these meetings, a complete record was put together and analyzed, including oral and written statements from 1,500 people, organizations and government agencies. Support for including the Chattooga in the National Wild and Scenic System was nearly unanimous. Remarkably, only three individuals and one private hunt club opposed the inclusion of the Chattooga in the Wild and Scenic River System.

When the responsibility for managing the Wild and Scenic River fell to the Forest Service in 1975, the Regional Forester assigned the responsibility for the administration of the Chattooga area to the Sumter National Forest, headquartered in Stumphouse Ranger station located on Highway 28 in Mountain Rest. Management prescribed by the Wild and Scenic Rivers Act began in the same year.

Management of the Wild and Scenic River

During preliminary studies, it became clear that certain portions of rivers, while not wild in the classic sense of true "wilderness," were nevertheless unique in character and worthy of protection in their own right. To allow for these varying degrees of wildness, the act provides for three classes of designation—wild, scenic, and recreation. The Chattooga has portions of each classification.

Sixty-eight percent of the Chattooga is classified as WILD, where management seeks to preserve the river and its immediate environment in a natural, wild and primitive condition while providing water-oriented recreation opportunities in a primitive setting. Five percent of the Chattooga is classified as SCENIC where management will enhance and maintain the high-quality scenery, provide river-oriented recreation and minimize impacts from existing roads and bridges that carry traffic across the corridor. Twenty-seven percent of the river is classified for RECREATION, in which management shall provide compatible outdoor recreational opportunities and water-oriented recreational facilities and utilize other resources which maintain or enhance the quality of wildlife, fisheries, scenic, or recreational values.

Today, recreational facilities within the corridor are for the most part primitive, and are intended to safeguard the wild character of the river environment from overdevelopment and uncontrolled human use. Use of motorized vehicles of any kind is prohibited within the corridor except on selected already existing roads. There are no major, developed campgrounds; above Highway 76, hiking trails traverse much of the corridor and help to disperse camping away from any one location.

Chattooga Plant Life

William Bartram, famous colonial naturalist and writer, traveled through the Chattooga watershed in the late eighteenth century. In his book, *The Travels of William Bartram*, he recounts his crossing of the Chattooga river:

> I traveled some miles over a varied situation of ground, exhibiting views of grand forests, dark detached groves, vales and meadows, as heretofore, and producing the like vegetable and other works of nature; the meadows affording exhuberant pasturage for cattle, and the bases of the encircling hills, flowering plants and fruitful strawberry beds; observed frequently ruins of the habitations or villages of the ancients. Crossed a delightful river, the main branch of the Tugilo [Chattooga], when I began to ascend again, first over swelling turfy ridges, varied with groves of stately forest trees; then ascending more steep and grassy hillsides, rested on top of mount Magnolia, which appeared to me to be the highest ridge of the Cherokee mountains, which separate the waters of the Savannah river from those of the Tanase [Tennessee].

The mountain forests of the Chattooga are a prime factor in the rich diversity of the river environment. The forest here is especially diverse, for the Chattooga gorge lies within a transition zone, where Appalachian forests dominated by hardwood species begin to grade into the oak/

hickory/pine mixed forests of the upper Piedmont. The Appalachian forest is an essentially deciduous forest type, characterized by many northern  ern hardwood species; this forest, sometimes referred to as the Appalachian Greenbelt, extends all the way to Maine and is, in fact, one of the most extensive hardwood ecosystems in the world. Some of the northern tree species that represent this great forest in and around the Chattooga gorge are actually holdovers from the Pleistocene Epoch, established in these mountains when the climate was more northern-like; now these species grow at the extreme southern limit of their range. Most of the Chattooga watershed now supports a medium to mature age second growth oak/pine forest with numerous northern cove hardwood species and hemlock, both present in the ravines and on well-watered slopes.

The original Chattooga forests, engendered and patiently shaped by the millennial forces of wind, water, ice, wildfire and drought, have undergone radical change in the historical era, both at the hand of nature and of man. Not many years ago the forests here and elsewhere in the southern Blue Ridge were a mixed oak/chestnut forest, but a blight earlier in this century effectively eliminated the American chestnut. At one time the Appalachian forests were probably one-quarter chestnut trees; some ridge tops held nothing but chestnuts trees, which attained ages upwards of five hundred years and grew to be a hundred feet tall. Since their virtual disappearance, various oaks such as red and white oak and especially chestnut oak have replaced the vanished American chestnut, as have tulip poplar, red maple and sourwood, among others.

Much of the human-wrought changes have unfortunately not been for the good. The little remaining virgin timber along the river and the intricate mosaic of old logging traces give some idea of the extent of past human disturbances in the area. The excesses of early logging practices as well as the burning and clearing of farmland inevitably degraded the magnificent primeval forest that survived in these mountains up until about the turn of the century. The disappearance of that age-old forest represents far more than the mere loss of its great trees to the saw mills. More important was the loss both of deep woods habitat and the amazingly rich species diversity of the original forests.

The gravity and full biological extent of these alterations in the forests are only now beginning to be understood. Fortunately, here in the Chattooga watershed, even though the forest has been significantly altered, enough flora and habitat survives in scattered, inaccessible places—usually in ravines where neither wildfire nor logging could reach—to at least remind us of the rich botanical heritage that has long since been lost elsewhere. However, to return its full, interactive richness found before the intrusion of Europeans, it would take several hundred years to recover if left undisturbed. The mountain forests of the Chattooga, though diminished, are still impressive, and offer us a unique opportunity to watch the natural progress of recovery as the forests heal from past woundings.

What might appear to the casual observer as a static environment—a uniform sea of trees—is actually a rich assemblage of natural communities made up of trees and plants, rocks and soil, and, of course, animals, all integrated into one living system of interconnecting components. This diversity results in a characteristic overlapping of forest habitats, where the boundaries between different forest communities may not always be distinct. Still, though the flora actually exists as a continuum that does not lend itself to simple classification, we can see some basic patterns in forest communities.

Some tree species are very shade intolerant; they may need all-day sun. Others grow well without direct sun altogether. Some species like the higher ridges where the drying effects of wind and sun are greatest; other vegetation needs the shelter of coves where high humidity helps protect against climatic extremes. Which trees grow in any one area is determined by specific site conditions such as elevation and climatic conditions, and also by its history of alteration by human or natural forces. Drier ridges and upper south-facing slopes in the Chattooga watershed will be dominated by shortleaf and Virginia pine, scarlet and chestnut oak. Cooler, wetter, more north-facing slopes, as well as coves and ravines are usually characterized by stands of hemlock, white pine and tulip poplar. On moderately moist ridges various species of oak and pine will dominate. Wetter habitats such as streamside areas will support alder, sycamore and cottonwood.

In addition to the trees, a great many different herbs and shrubs grow in the forest communities here. Mountain laurel, mountain magnolia, dog hobble and rhododendron, all evergreen shrubs, are present. Non-evergreen shrubs include flame azalea, dogwood, horse sugar, witch hazel, sweet pepperbush, wild hydrangea, spicewood, chinquapin, yellow root and strawberry shrub, to name but a few.

Wildflowers

The diverse nature of the forests here accompanied by a corresponding diversity of soil types greatly influences the number and variety of wildflowers. The Chattooga gorge, while not as rich botanically as it once was, is nevertheless blessed with many varieties of wild orchids, ferns,

lilies, trilliums and violets, among others. Some idea of the plant diversity in this region may be had if we note that the Chattooga, two tropical filmy ferns occur—the bristly and the dwarf filmy fern—just a few miles from the crest of the Eastern Continental Divide where we might find Arctic lichens clinging to the high rocks.

A number of plants found in the Chattooga watershed are PETS species—Proposed, Endangered, Threatened and Sensitive species—as, for instance, the Mountain Camellia. Once considered to be one of our rarest shrubs, it is fortunately somewhat more common than originally thought. The Mountain Camellia flowers in a large white bloom similar to that of a dogwood or a magnolia. The Shortia plant, the Oconee Bells, is one of our rarest plants. Though locally abundant in some places in the Chattoga gorges, Shortia is nevertheless not native to the Chattooga gorge at all; all current populations are transplants. Other PETS species in the Chattooga watershed include the small whorled pogonia, the Piedmont strawberry, Umbrella leaf, Fraser's Loosestrife, and American Ginseng, as well as the climbing fern and the maidenhair spleenwort.

In the past few decades, many natural environments of plants and wildlife have fallen victim to urban expansion and industrialization. Many

Some Chattooga Area Plants

Common Name	Latin Name	Blooms
bluets	(Houstonia spp.)	February-April
trailing arbutus	(Epigaea repens)	February-May
bloodroot	(Sanguinaria canadensis)	March-May
bird foot violet	(viola pedata)	March-June
Oconee Bells	(Shortia galicifolia)	March-April
common blue violet	(Viola spp.)	March-June
trout lily	(Erythronium americanus)	March-June
Hepatica	(Hepatica acutiloba)	March-June
wood anemone	(Anemone quinquefolia)	March-May
rue anemone	(Thalictrum thalcitroides)	March-May
sessile trillium	(Trillium cuneatum)	March-May
dwarf crested iris	(Iris cristata)	April-May
jack-in-pulpit	(Arisaema triphyllum)	April-June
wild geranium	(Geranium maculatum)	April-June
bellwort	(Uvularia spp.)	April-June
dog hobble	(Leucothoe axillaris)	late April-May
Vasey's trillium	(Trillium vasey)	April-June
showy orchis	(Orchis spectabilis)	April-June
yellow lady's slipper	(Cypripedium pubescens)	April-August
foam flower	(Tiarella cordifolia)	April-June
sweet white violet	(Viola blanda)	April-May
great white trillium	(Trillium grandifolia)	April-June
painted trillium	(Trillium undulatem)	April-June
mayapple	(Podophyllum peltatum)	April-June
false Solomon's seal	(Smilacina racemose)	May-June
Solomon's seal	(Polygonatum biflorum)	May-June
flame azalea	(Rh. calendulaceum)	May-June
galax	(Galax aphylla)	May-June
mountain laurel	(Kalmia latifolia)	late May-June
rosebay rhododendron	(Rhododendron maximum)	June-July
partridge berry	(Mitchella repens)	June-July
spotted wintergreen	(Chimaphila maculata)	June-August
Indian pipe	(Monotropa uniflora)	June-Sept.
rattlesnake plaintain	(Goodyera repens)	July-August
fire pink	(Silene virginica)	late-spring

of our deep woods habitats—critical to the survival of some reclusive species—have been fragmented by roads or abusive logging practices such as clearcutting. Fortunately, attitudes toward delicate ecosystems are changing as their obvious benefit to humans, aesthetic and scientific, become more apparent. Nevertheless, extinction of native plant species continues world-wide, even before being catalogued by science. The Chattooga River corridor is all the more valuable to us precisely because it can be a haven for species, insignificant or otherwise, which have little chance of surviving the habitat disruptions that marr unprotected areas. A list of some wildflowers that can be found in the Chattooga watershed is on the preceeding page.

Chattooga Wildlife

Because the Chattooga River corridor is not subject to the range of disturbances that often mar adjacent and outlying landscapes, it serves as an important haven for wildlife. It is, even today, relatively rich in animal species, though we do well to remember that it is not so rich as it once was.

A British officer detached to Fort Prince George in the early 1760s wrote in his journal of the "vast howling of wolves" that disconcerted him one spring evening. (Fort Prince George, situated in Keowee valley just east of Chattooga ridge, was then a miserable, dangerous outpost of the British empire, two hundred and fifty miles from Charles Town.) Though wolves could still be found in some remote areas of the Carolinas as late as the early 1900s, both the Red and the Gray wolf have long since disappeared from the Chattooga watershed. Gone with the wolf is the Eastern Buffalo, the last of which disappeared from the Carolinas in the 1760s, such that John Bartram, pioneer botanist and father of William Bartram, could bemoan the "heaps of the white gnawed bones of the ancient buffalo," which he reported were "once so very numerous, [but] not at this day to be found in this part of the country." Also gone is the elk, which succumbed to hunting pressures by the late 1700s.

Somewhat later, by the beginning of this century, the mountain populations of the White-tailed deer had been hunted out, and with them went the mountain lion as well as the beaver. In the last two decades, both deer and beaver have been reintroduced and have flourished. However, too many other former members of the Chattooga's wild mammal heritage are gone forever, nor are we likely to see them reintroduced in our lifetime.

Despite the sad loss of these important species, the Chattooga is nevertheless one of the last best remaining primitive river environments in the Southeast, with literally thousands of invertebrate species present as well as many species of mammal, bird, reptile, amphibian and fish. Its still-rich faunal diversity makes the watershed an often rewarding place for seeing wildlife, though the rugged, steep terrain and the many dense rhododendron and laurel "slicks" can make the enterprise a challenging one. Many if not most mammals are nocturnal and thus not easily seen. Small nut-eating animals like squirrels and chipmunks tend to be more obvious than other small mammals, like the deer mouse and the White-footed mouse. These last two, though seldom seen, are abundant and are important sources of food for predatory species like owls, weasels, raccoons, bobcats and foxes. Cottontails, also important in the food pyramid, are plentiful in the area, as are quail and dove.

Beaver, muskrat, mink, opossum and woodchucks are all found in the Chattooga drainage; beaver seem to be doing well and expanding their range such that their dam building has become a problem in some of the smaller tributaries.

Black bear are present in the Chattooga drainage. Most of these are transplants. Bear require large contiguous blocks of land for range, something on the order of thirty-five to fifty thousand acres. The National Forest lands surrounding the Chattooga have the potential to be prime bear habitat, but unfortunately the management of the three area forests has not been sufficiently consolidated to protect the needed habitat. Most black bear seen in the Chattooga area are probably migrating back and forth across Chattooga Ridge from the nucleus of their range—the mountainous, inaccessible region north of Lake Jocassee.

Fully three dozen other mammal species inhabit the Chattooga area, including numerous species of bats, moles, rats and mice. Both the Striped and the Eastern Spotted skunk are present, the latter of which is considered to be rare. The Indiana bat, a federally endangered species, is documented in the Chattooga area, and two species are candidates for inclusion on the federal list of endangered species—the southern Appalachian eastern woodrat and the Appalachian cottontail rabbit.

Avifauna

Bird life abounds in the Chattooga watershed, as it does throughout the escarpment gorge region, a result of the rich diversity of floral habitats dispersed over a wide range of elevations. Between the upper and lower extremes of elevations, one may find an amazing variety of forests and

plant communities—oak/hickory forests, oak/pine forests, streamside and flood plain forests as well as open areas like old fields and cut-over forests—each home to distinctive bird species. Most bird species will be found near areas that best suit them, though some are more tolerant of habitat variations than others, and so occupy a range of forest and plant communities.

In forests dominated by oak/hickory or oak/pine associations one can spot the Carolina Wren, Solitary and Red-eyed Vireo, Scarlet Tanager, Eastern Phoebe and in the upper reaches of the watershed the Rose-breasted Grosbeak. One can also spot several owls (the Great-horned, Screech and Barred Owl), hawks (Red-tailed and Red Shouldered hawk) woodpeckers (Common Flicka and Red-bellied Woodpecker) as well as a number of warblers.

Forests dominated by pines are most often found on dry ridges or steep exposed slopes where the soil is rocky and poor. Bird life may be less diverse, especially if a single tree species dominates, as in areas planted for timber production. However, where the pine forest has a rich understory, birds are more apt to be seen. Some birds likely to be present include the Eastern Screech Owl, Blue Jay, Wood Thrush, Northern Cardinal, and in lower pine-dominated forests, the Pine Warbler.

Some birds like the cool, shaded streamsides in the area, where hemlock and white pine usually dominate, towering over understories thick with rhododendron and mountain laurel. Canada Warblers, Blackburnian Warblers, the Louisiana Waterthrush and the relatively rare (in this area) Swainson's Warbler use these streamside areas as nesting grounds. At the upper end of the watershed one might find birds normally associated with more northern climes, as for instance the Golden-crowned Kinglet and Red-breasted Nuthatch.

The relative inaccessibility of much of the gorge makes it good wild turkey country, especially for nesting, since turkey will abandon nests disturbed in any way. Perhaps more than most animals, the turkey is reliant upon the oak-hickory forest's abundance of acorns and hickory nuts. However, if the mast is not good, turkey may also consume insects, salamanders, toads, crustaceans, lizards and snakes, in addition to wild grapes and other berry fruits that might be available. The wild turkey has made a significant come back in recent years, though its present numbers nowhere near approximate the flocks of thousands that early records indicate once inhabited the eastern forests. Wild turkey can sometimes be seen flying across the river, especially when they are startled by a quiet paddler appearing unannounced around a bend. Ruffed Grouse are also present, and like the turkey, take advantage of the dense understory.

Certain other river birds worthy of note can be seen with relative frequency in the lower sections of the watershed, depending upon the season. Both the Green-backed Heron (Little Green Heron) and the Great Blue Heron occur along the river and can be found along tributaries. Belted Kingfishers are common, as are various swallows and flycatchers along the river margins. Wood Ducks and Mallards are fairly common, though not in great numbers; they are more evident during migration periods. Canada Geese also occur on the Chattooga during migration.

Osprey, or Fish Hawks as they are sometimes called, use the Chattooga corridor during migration; early spring is a good time to see them as they stopover. Southern Bald Eagles have been sighted along the river and around Lake Tugaloo. Both the Southern Bald Eagle and the Osprey are listed by the USFS Land and Resource Management Plan as transient species. The Osprey is on the South Carolina state list of Threatened and Endangered Species; the Southern Bald Eagle is on the Federal list. Another endangered species, the magnificent Peregrine Falcon, is known to breed on rocky crags in the Southern Appalachians. Peregrine Falcons are now hacked (reintroduced) on Whiteside Mountain and around Lake Jocassee and the bird has been spotted along the Chattooga as well.

Because the Chattooga lies within a major migration corridor, birding is especially good in the spring, when a veritable tide of passerine songbirds moves through the area—including some twenty-five species of warbler—all of which follow the budding of the trees up the gorge and the corresponding insect hatch. The Warbler's journey through the Chattooga country is indicative of the perilous vicissitudes of all migratory birds. After leaving their wintering grounds in Central and South America, many warblers cross the Gulf of Mexico and then moves northward with the emerging spring to nest on the high slopes above the escarpment gorges. Now, however, according to some biologists, this living tide of neo-tropical migrants is increasingly in jeopardy as tropical deforestation destroys more and more of the wintering grounds of many birds that breed in North America. Some biologists put the decline at fifty or even seventy percent, with some fifty species at risk—thrushes, warblers and vireos particularly—as well as flycatchers and tanagers. Where fifty years ago the woods were full of songbirds, there are now, in some places, only trickles. John Terborgh's *Where Have all the Birds Gone* is a good reference for anyone wanting to know more about this threat to our neo-tropical migrants.

This section has offered only a cursory description of the variety of bird species to be found in the Chattooga watershed. To get a more exacting guide, turn to *Birds of the Carolinas*, by Eloise F. Potter, James F. Parnell and Robert P. Teulings, or *Birds of the Blue Ridge Mountains*, by Marcus B. Simpson, Jr.

Reptiles and Amphibians

The warm climate of the Chattooga watershed makes the area prime snake habitat, with more than two dozen species present. The Northern Water snake is most often encountered on the river; the Eastern Garter snake perhaps most commonly in the surrounding forests. Other snakes include the Eastern King snake, the Northern ringneck snake, Northern Black racer, Eastern Hognose, Common Black Rat snake, Corn snake, and, among others, the Eastern Milk snake. There are only two snakes in the Chattooga watershed that are poisonous: the Timber rattler and the Copperhead.

The warm temperatures and high humidity and rainfall make the Chattooga gorge some of the finest salamander country in the world. Of the almost three dozen species that inhabit the Southern Appalachians, at least a dozen different species are found in the Chattooga gorge, including one—the husky shovel-nosed salamander—found nowhere else. Among others occurring here are the black-bellied and the seal salamander, the Highlands and the Carolina Spring salamander. The very large Eastern Hellebender, native to warmer, low altitude streams and reaching almost thirty inches in length, is reported to be present in the lower reaches of the Chattooga gorge, though no sitings have been documented.

Eastern Spotted Newts, both in their aquatic and terrestrial forms, are common in Chattooga gorge. Over a dozen species of frogs and toads are present, including the American toad and Southern toad, the Gray tree frog, the Bull frog, Southern Leopard and Wood frog. There are at least four species of turtle here, including the Eastern box turtle and the common snapping turtle. Lizards and skinks, including the Green Anole, the Northern Fence lizard, the Southeastern Five-lined, the Broadhead and the Coal skink, can be found in and around the Chattooga watershed.

Chattooga Fish Species

As might be expected, because of the precipitous nature of the Chattooga, most species indigenous to the watershed are fast-water loving fish. Though more than twenty species of fish can be found in the watershed, including smallmouth and redeye bass, various sunfishes, chubs, darters, dace, shiners and suckers, the Chattooga is perhaps best known as a trout stream. It is in fact known to be a quite good trout stream despite its heavy use and popularity.

In the earliest days, the Chattooga's only native trout, the Brook trout, were plentiful enough in the southern mountains to be relied upon as dependable trail food, and, for a while, as a main food source for forts,  homesteads and settlements. This plenitude was short-lived, however, as settlers and then timber companies plowed and denuded the land, starting in the nineteenth and continuing into the twentieth century. The effects of plowing and cutting the land–siltation and increased water temperature–forced the brook trout into higher and more remote areas. Today its range is markedly diminished and is found in only a dozen or so streams in this area. With the decreasing numbers of native Brook, eager anglers wanted a replacement fish. Eventually Rainbow and later Brown trout were introduced, fish more tolerant to the altered water habitat.

Industrial abuses have not been the sole cause of trout stream loss. The outstanding natural beauty of the Southern Appalachians draws people, and with people come more roads, more resorts and sub-divisions, the construction of any of which can silt in streams and denude stream banks, eventually raising the water temperature beyond that tolerable to cold-water loving trout. The proliferation of small ponds built on Chattooga tributaries is becoming a critical problem in sustaining viable trout habitat. These ponds, many of them associated with golf courses in and around Highlands and Cashiers, have a cumulative effect that adds up to a significant warming of the trout waters overall. In South Carolina especially, trout waters have been so diminished by half a century of habitat degradation that environmental factors are already at the limit of what trout can tolerate.

In spite of these disturbances, the fish themselves, in natural competition with each other, have reached something of a natural balance in southern mountain streams. The Rainbow, like the Brook trout, prefers cool, clear, cascading streams , though it is more aggressive than the native Brookies. In streams where both fish occur, the rainbow usually wins out; the Brook trout is then usually found only in small headwater streams (in South Carolina almost always above 1500 feet) often above some natural barrier to browns and rainbows—a waterfall, for instance. The Brown trout generally likes bigger, slower streams with an abundance of minnows, though it does mix with rainbows in fast, clear, medium-size streams.

Recreation on the Chattooga

Use of the Chattooga increases every year and is likely to intensify as more and more people discover the beauty and unique wild character of this place. As demand for the Chattooga experience increases, so must each individual's commitment to protect the river's wild nature. Visiting the river, especially traveling on it and camping overnight, implies special concerns and techniques; we need to be sure that any changes we make upon the character of the wild river are kept to a bare minimum.

Here are a few ways to lessen your impact in this pristine country:

- Stay on designated trails. Do not by pass switch-backs.
- Camp only in designated and established areas.
- Pack it in; Pack it out.
- Avoid campfires by using stoves. If you must have a fire, use established fire rings.
- When nature calls, use existing outhouses. When these are unavailable, avoid areas near streams and creeks. Preferably locate an area where the humus is thick. Bury all human waste, but pack out sanitary napkins and tampons.

For more information on low impact camping, read Bruce Hampton and David Cole's book, *Soft Paths*, a publication of the National Outdoor Leadership School.

The five major access points along the Chattooga include the Highway 76 bridge between Long Creek, SC and Clayton, GA; the Earl's Ford Road on either side of the river (in SC on FS 196 near Mountain Rest; in Georgia, a rough, often muddy and sometimes impassable road off Warwoman Road); Highway 28, or Russell bridge; the "new" Burrell's Ford Road that turns off Highway 28 just before the Russell Bridge; and Bull Pen Road off SC 107 south of US 64 near Cashiers, NC.

It should also be noted that travel on or around the Chattooga, whether fishing, hiking or whitewater paddling, assumes certain levels of ability and preparedness that must not be ignored. Sudden thunderstorms can and do come on suddenly, creating conditions perfect for hypothermia, even in the middle of summer, or an accident in the backcountry can leave you in dire circumstances if unprepared. Don't venture out without at least food, water and a first aid kit.

Hiking and Camping

Many miles of trail traverse the Chattooga corridor and adjacent Forest Service and private lands. Some of these trails link up with longer, more extensive trail systems in the Sumter, Chattahoochee and Nantahala National Forests, making multi-day trips in or through the corridor possible as well. The hiking possibilities are virtually limitless.

Permits are not required for hiking but are required for camping on any federal land outside the Ellicott Rock Wilderness or the Chattooga Wild and Scenic corridor. (These permits are available at the Stumphouse Ranger Station, north of Walhalla on Highway 28.) Within the Chattooga corridor, permit-free camping is permitted anywhere except within fifty feet of any river or tributary and a quarter-mile from any road. (Some additional areas in Ellicott Rock Wilderness prohibit camping.) Numerous camping sites along the river are marked with small signs. Though campers may select an undesignated site if it meets Forest Service regulations, it is always best to camp in areas already impacted by campsites rather than to construct new campsites and needlessly destroy vegetation. No-trace camping is strongly encouraged to minimize damage to the river environment.

The Burrel's Ford camping area provides tables, water, campsites and toilets. The area is closed to vehicles and is reached by a 350-yard foot trail. The only "primitive" camping areas open to vehicle access are Long

Bottom Ford on the main river and on the West Fork in Georgia. Trash containers and toilets are provided.

Trails

The hiking trails along and near the Chattooga provide a number of options for anglers, backpackers and day hikers. Trails are usually located away from the river to reduce contact between various users and to provide more solitude and otherwise enhance the river experience.

Of historical note, there were at one time at least three Indian trails crossing the Chattooga, according to a modern map compilation. One trail ascended Chattooga Ridge from the large Cherokee towns on Keowee, 20 miles to the east, and crossed the Chattooga near present-day Burrel's Ford. Another trail ascended Chattooga Ridge from the same area, crossing the Chattooga at Earl's Ford and winding up Warwoman Creek on its way to Rabun Gap and the Tennessee basin. A third major trail appears to have come up from the Cherokee Lower Town of Tugaloo, on the Tugaloo River, and followed the route of present-day Highway 76, crossing the Chattooga at Rogue's Ford (site of Highway 76 bridge).

The following short inventory of trails provides some idea of the range of hiking experiences available; the list is not comprehensive nor is it intended to substitute for a good trail guide. A good guide to the area is available at Stumphouse Ranger Station and at Chattooga River Outfitter Headquarters. Also available is the USFS Chattooga Wild and Scenic River map, which provides valuable information for both floaters and hikers. However, the *Georgia Conservancy's Guide To The North Georgia Mountains*, edited by Fred Brown and Nell Jones is the best resource for hikers.

(1) Chattooga River Loop Trail (NC)
A .5 mile loop trail beginning at the Chattooga parking lot and ending at the Bull Pen Bridge.

(2) Chattooga River Trail (NC)
Beginning at Bull Pen Bridge, extends 1.0 mile northward along the river's west bank. An additional 2 miles remain to be built. The Chattooga above Bull Pen Bridge is rugged and wild, closed to boats, and notable for the Chattooga Cliffs.

(3) Spoon Auger Falls Trail (SC)

Begins at Burrel's Ford campground parking lot and extends roughly 1/2 mile north to Spoon Auger Falls. Trail continues on another 1.5 miles to intersect with Chattooga River Trail.

(4) King Creek Falls Trail (SC)

Begins at Burrell's Ford Campground and extends .5 mile south to King Creek Falls. The stream is notable for its dense stands of hardwood; the falls for its height and lovely pool beneath.

(5) Foothills National Recreation Trail (SC)

Enters the Chattooga river corridor at Licklog Creek and extends 8.7 miles to Medlin Bridge where it exits the corridor bound for Highway 107. Much of this trail coincides with the Chattooga River Trail. Skirts southern edge but does not penetrate the Ellicott Rock Wilderness. This long, sometimes rugged and remote SC trail extends from Table Rock State Park to Oconee State Park, crossing the lower ends of several of the Blue Ridge Escarpment gorges. A Guide to the Foothills Trail, published by the Foothills Trail Conference is available. For more information contact Foothills Trail Conference, P.O. Box 3041, Greenville, S. C. 29602.

(6) Bartram National Recreation Trail (GA)

Enters the river corridor at Dick's Creek and extends 10 miles to Highway 28 following the same right-of-way as the Chattooga River Trail. This long trail commemorates botanist William Bartram's famous journey through this area. Extends from NC Highway 106 above Blue Valley through the Chattooga corridor to SC Highway 107 and Long Mountain. For more information contact Bartram Trail Association, Rt. 3, Box 406, Sylva, N.C. 28779.

(7) Earl's Ford Portage Trail(SC)

Major portage trail, begins at Earl's Ford parking lot, extends 450 yards to the river.

(8) Sandy Ford Portage Trail (SC)

Minor portage trail, extends 500 yards from Sandy Ford Road to the river.

(9) Fall Creek Portage Trail (SC)
Major portage trail extending .5 mile from FS 769 to the river. Notoriously long as a put-in trail.

(10) Dick's Creek Trail (GA)
Extends from FS 9 about .5 mile to the river.

(11) Lick Log Trail (GA)
Extends .1 mile from the Bartram Trail to Dick's Creek Falls.

(12) Thrift's Ferry Trail (SC) (Tilly Branch Trail)
Major portage trail extending 500 yards from end of FS 795, off Highway 76.

(13) Bull Sluice Portage Trail (SC)
Major asphalt-surfaced portage trail extending from Highway 76 Parking Lot to the river. An unpaved fork goes to Bull Sluice rapid.

(14) Chattooga Ridge Trail (SC, GA)
Begins at NC/SC state line and runs 17.3 miles downstream to the Highway 28 Bridge, crosses the Chattooga and runs another 20 miles to the Highway 76 Bridge. Portions of the Bartram and Foothills Trails also follow the Chattooga Trail. Approximately 3.5 miles of this trail lie within Ellicott Rock Wilderness. Burrel's Ford campground is the only developed camping area. The trail is complete except for a footbridge across the West Fork in GA.

(15) Sutton Hole Trail (GA)
Extends from FS 290-A about .3 mile to the river. Riverside campsite is used by one Chattooga River outfitter for overnight trips in season.

(16) Woodall Shoals Portage (SC)
Major portage trail extending from Woodall Shoals Parking Lot 330 yards to the river. Primitive campsites are available. Campsite used by one Chattooga river outfitter for overnight trips in season.

(17) Camp Creek Trail (GA)
Extends from FS 511 about .5 mile to the river. Last portage trail above gorge of the Five Falls.

(18) Raven Rock Trail (GA)
Extends from FS 511-B about .8 mile to the river.

(19) Opossum Creek Trail (SC)
A new trail to replace one wiped out by the 1994 Palm Sunday tornado. Extends from Turkey Ridge Road about two miles to junction of Opossum Creek and Chattooga.

Ellicott Rock Wilderness Area

This primitive tract of 9,012 acres is comprised of wild mountain land that surrounds Ellicott Rock, the riverside survey mark indicating where Georgia, South Carolina and North Carolina come together. This small but rich wilderness first began as a small scenic area in 1966 then achieved National Wilderness status in 1975, thereby garnering the full weight of protection granted in the 1960 Wilderness Protection Act. No horses, motorbikes or bicycles are permitted here. The Forest Service seeks a 2,000 acre addition to this area in the Sumter National Forest.

There is considerable topographical relief in this small but remote area, including two mountains over three thousand feet: Red Side in Georgia and Fork Mountain in South Carolina. Fork Mountain is the second highest point in South Carolina. Trails listed below are in Ellicott Rock Wilderness.

(A) Ellicott Rock Trail (NC)
Begins at Bull Pen Road west of the Chattooga and runs 3.5 miles southwest to a ford 50 yards above Ellicott Rock, then extends 3.5 miles west to FS 5441 near Scotsman's Creek.

(B) Bad Creek Trail (NC)
Originates at Bull Pen Road east of the Chattooga and intersects at roughly 2.5 miles with the Sloan Bridge Trail, thereafter switchbacks steeply 1.5 miles down to the Chattooga. Ellicott Rock is just downstream.

(C) East Fork Trail (SC) (Fish Hatchery Trail)
Begins at the Chattooga Picnic Area and descends 2.5 miles to the river. This trail is heavily used, especially the first portion, which is a loop trail through the magnificent specimens of old growth hemlock that make the area so appealing.

(D) Chattooga River Trail (SC)
See above listing. Approximately 3.5 miles of this long trail lie within Ellicott Rock Wilderness.

(E) Sloan Bridge Trail (SC)
Also known as the Fork Mountain Trail, extends from SC 107 into the wilderness about 6.5 miles to Bad Creek trail, then proceeds another 1.5 mile to the river and Ellicott Rock.

Whitewater Rafting

The Chattooga is a beautiful place to see from the water, whether in a private group or with a commercial outfitter. There are fourteen parking lots that provide access to the river, with floating limited to the twenty-six-mile section below the Highway 28 bridge and the lower four-mile section of the West Fork in Georgia.

Because the river upstream of Lake Tugaloo achieved Wild and Scenic River protection before it could be inundated, the Chattooga remains free-flowing. Fed only by rainwater, the Chattooga is subject to fairly wide seasonal fluctuations in flow rate, with the lowest levels generally occurring in late summer and fall. During low water periods the commercial outfitters may use smaller rafts, shorten their trips or move them down river as water flow dictates.

Conversely, the river can get quite high. Chattooga whitewater, especially Section IV, presents potentially lethal hazards to any private boater or rafter who does not know or appreciate the difficulty and power of the river. The vast majority of fatalities on this river have been people who did not know or care to heed the warning signs at the put-in points. Caution is always best heeded.

Chattooga River Outfitters

Nantahala Outdoor Center
13077 Hwy. 19 West
Bryson City, NC 28713-9114
(800) 232-7238
(803) 647-9014

Southeastern Expeditions
2936-H N. Druid Hills Road
Atlanta, GA 30329
(800) 868-7238
(404) 329-0433

Wildwater Ltd.
P.O. Box 309
Long Creek, SC 29658
(800) 451-9972
(803) 647-9587

Sections II, III, and IV offer increasingly challenging whitewater. Section II offers mostly flat water, with an occasional Class 1 or 2 rapid. The largest rapid, Big Shoals, is Class 2. The Highway 28 bridge and the Forest Service area one mile downriver (on Highway 28) are popular put-in spots.

Section III runs fourteen miles long and is more demanding than Section II. Numerous Class 2 to 3 rapids like Dick's Creek, Second Ledge, the Narrows and Painted Rock Rapid punctuate Section III's fine mix of fast and slow water, with the final rapid, Bull Sluice (Class 4), presenting either the biggest challenge of the day for those that choose to run it, or an easy walk around the right side for those who do not. Typical put-ins on this section can be made at Earl's or Sandy Ford, Fall Creek and Thrifts Ferry.

The seven-mile long Section IV offers challenging, more technical whitewater for paddlers in good physical condition and with Class 4 whitewater experience under their belt. This stretch starts off beguilingly easy with several Class 3 rapids like Surfing Rapid, Screaming Left Turn and Rock Jumble before it begins to drop in earnest at Woodall Shoals. It should be noted that this most dangerous hydraulic on the river can be "cheated" on the right side at sufficient flows or walked around on the left anytime. Seven Foot Falls, just downstream, marks the beginning of the big drops, which culminate in the Five Falls, five successive Class 4 and 5 rapids dropping at a rate in excess of two hundred feet per mile: Entrance or First Fall, Corkscrew, Crack-in-the-Rock, Jawbone and Sock'em Dog. Section IV ends in the quiet waters of Lake Tugalo, an undeveloped and relatively remote hydroelectric impoundment built on the steep lower Chattooga in the 1920s. Typical put-ins on this section include the Highway 76 bridge and Woodall Shoals Road.

Fishing

Trout fishing is best above the Highway 28 bridge but is reasonably good for most of the river's length, though summer's hot days raise water temperatures in the lower reaches of the river to the limits of what most trout will tolerate. The only trout thought to be native to the system is the brookie. Rainbow and brown trout have been introduced and by now some naturally reproducing populations of both species are present. Nevertheless, stocking of hatchery-reared fish is necessary because of the river's heavy use. Brook trout have not been stocked here for about a decade, but in the more inaccessible reaches of the river's feeder streams a native population of brook trout survives. There is no stocking in the Ellicott Rock Wilderness.

The areas around the five major access points naturally receive the heaviest use, but fishing is also good in the Chattooga's many small tributaries. The East Fork, which flows through the Ellicott Rock Wilderness off SC 107 near the Walhalla Fish Hatchery, is known as a very good brown trout stream. (The East Fork's superlative fishing might simply be due to nutrient-rich discharge from the Walhalla Fish Hatchery.) The West Fork and its three headwater streams, Overflow, Holcomb and Big Creeks, are also all superb trout resources. The lower West Fork is readily accessible since it parallels GA 28 for about two miles before its confluence with the Chattooga. Its upper reaches, including the wild, rugged feeder streams mentioned above, are accessible from FS 86, the Overflow Creek Road, which turns off Warwoman Road 14 miles east of Clayton.

"Catch and Release" trout fishing is not required but is encouraged. Above Ellicott's Rock a North Carolina license is required; south of the North Carolina state line either a Georgia or a South Carolina license suffices. At present trout stamps are not required.

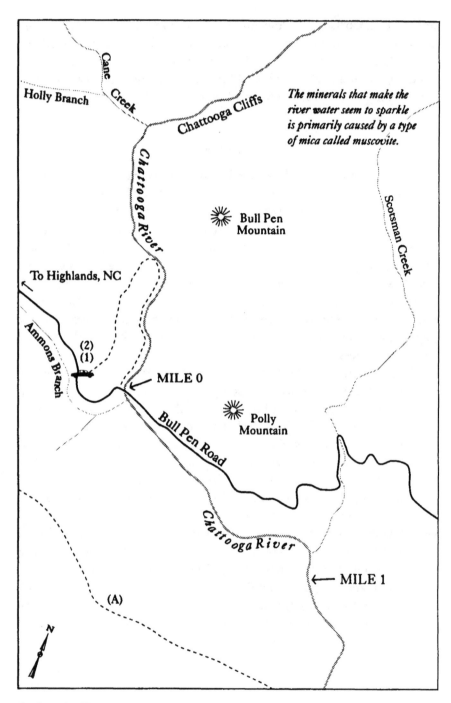

The minerals that make the river water seem to sparkle is primarily caused by a type of mica called muscovite.

Cane Creek

Holly Branch

Chattooga Cliffs

Chattooga River

Bull Pen Mountain

Scotsman Creek

To Highlands, NC

Ammons Branch

(2)
(1)

MILE 0

Bull Pen Road

Polly Mountain

Chattooga River

MILE 1

(A)

N

Guide to the Chattooga River–50

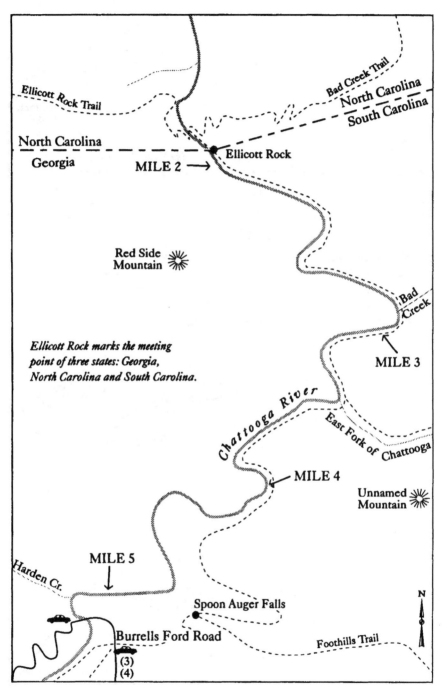

Ellicott Rock Trail

Bad Creek Trail

North Carolina
South Carolina

North Carolina
Georgia

MILE 2 →

Ellicott Rock

Red Side
Mountain

*Ellicott Rock marks the meeting
point of three states: Georgia,
North Carolina and South Carolina.*

Bad
Creek

MILE 3

Chattooga River

East Fork of Chattooga

MILE 4

Unnamed
Mountain

MILE 5

Harden Cr.

Spoon Auger Falls

Burrells Ford Road

Foothills Trail

N

(3)
(4)

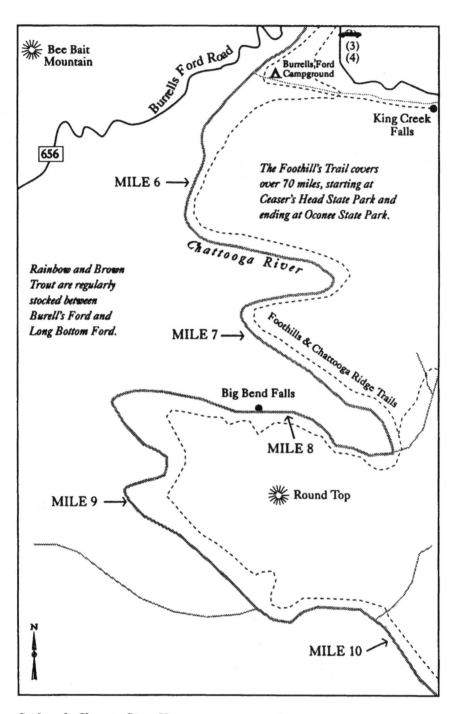

Bee Bait Mountain

Burrells Ford Road

(3)
(4)

Burrells Ford
Campground

King Creek
Falls

656

MILE 6 →

The Foothill's Trail covers
over 70 miles, starting at
Ceaser's Head State Park and
ending at Oconee State Park.

Chattooga River

Rainbow and Brown
Trout are regularly
stocked between
Burell's Ford and
Long Bottom Ford.

MILE 7 →

Foothills & Chattooga Ridge Trails

Big Bend Falls

MILE 8

Round Top

MILE 9 →

N

MILE 10 →

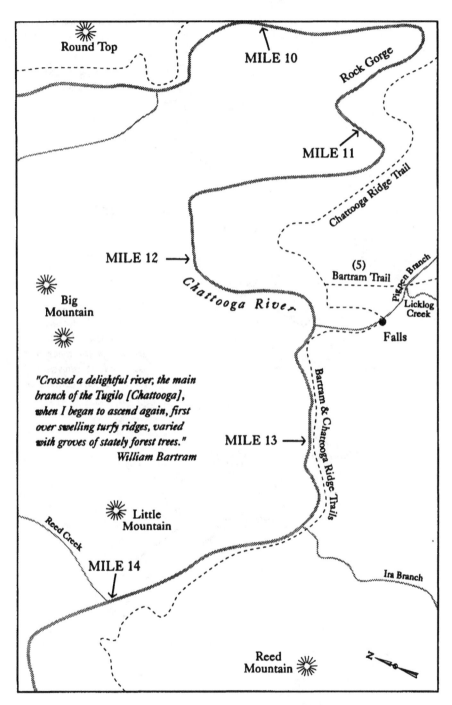

Round Top

MILE 10

Rock Gorge

MILE 11

Chattooga Ridge Trail

MILE 12 →

Chattooga River

(5)
Bartram Trail

Pigeon Branch

Licklog
Creek

Big
Mountain

Falls

"Crossed a delightful river, the main
branch of the Tugilo [Chattooga],
when I began to ascend again, first
over swelling turfy ridges, varied
with groves of stately forest trees."
William Bartram

MILE 13 →

Bartram & Chattooga Ridge Trails

Reed Creek

Little
Mountain

MILE 14

Ira Branch

Reed
Mountain

N

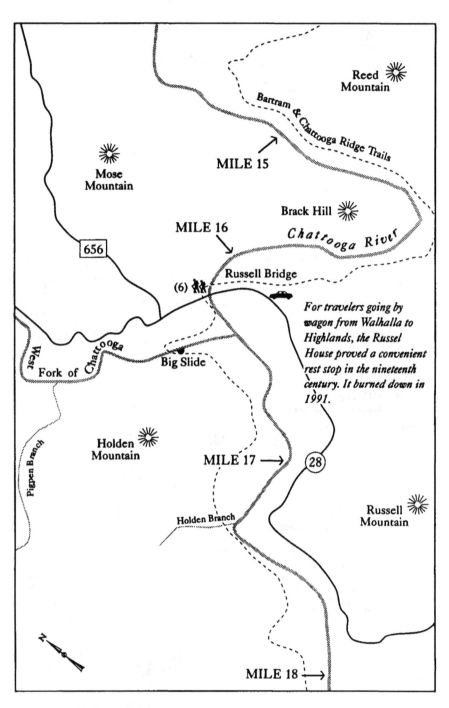

Reed Mountain

Bartram & Chattooga Ridge Trails

MILE 15

Mose Mountain

Brack Hill

MILE 16

Chattooga River

656

Russell Bridge

(6)

For travelers going by wagon from Walhalla to Highlands, the Russel House proved a convenient rest stop in the nineteenth century. It burned down in 1991.

West Fork of *Chattooga*

Big Slide

Pigpen Branch

Holden Mountain

MILE 17 →

28

Russell Mountain

Holden Branch

N

MILE 18 →

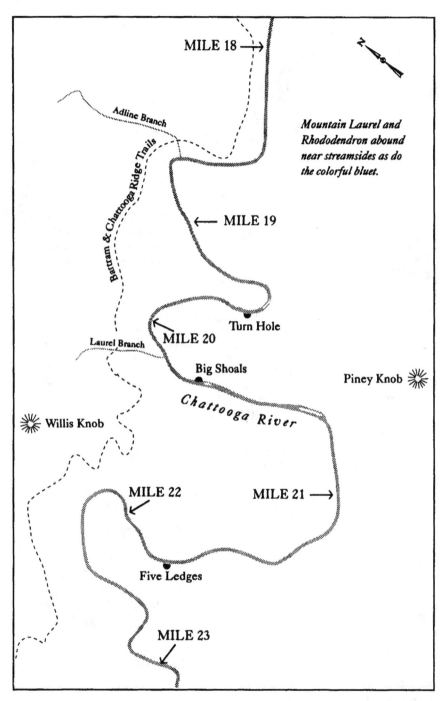

MILE 18 →

N

Mountain Laurel and Rhododendron abound near streamsides as do the colorful bluet.

Adline Branch

Bartram & Chattooga Ridge Trails

← MILE 19

Turn Hole

← MILE 20

Laurel Branch

Big Shoals

Piney Knob ☼

Chattooga River

☼ Willis Knob

MILE 22
↙

MILE 21 →

Five Ledges

MILE 23
↙

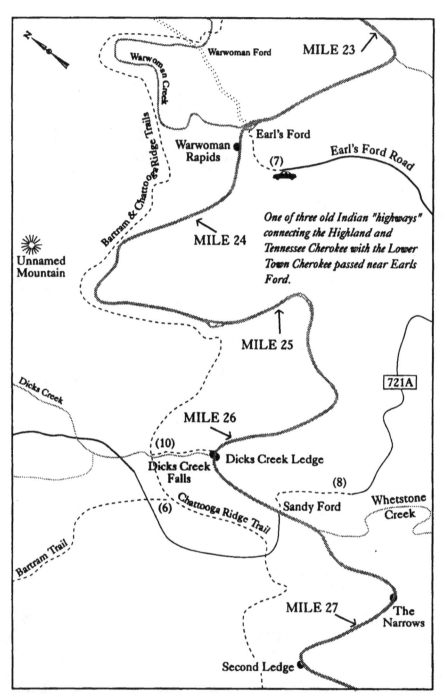

One of three old Indian "highways" connecting the Highland and Tennessee Cherokee with the Lower Town Cherokee passed near Earls Ford.

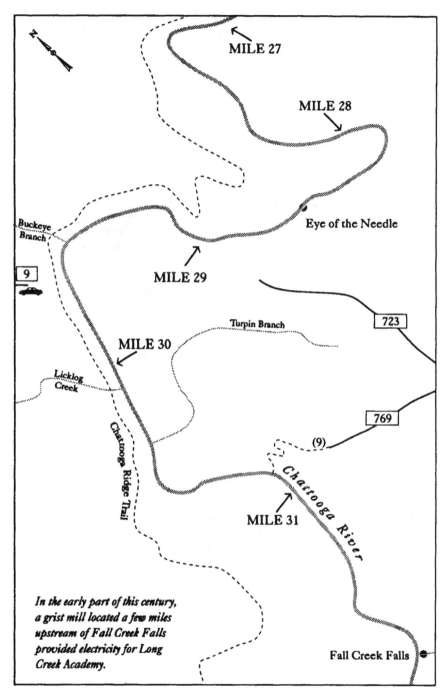

MILE 27

MILE 28

Eye of the Needle

Buckeye
Branch

9

MILE 29

723

Turpin Branch

MILE 30

Licklog
Creek

769

(9)

Chattooga Ridge Trail

Chattooga River

MILE 31

*In the early part of this century,
a grist mill located a few miles
upstream of Fall Creek Falls
provided electricity for Long
Creek Academy.*

Fall Creek Falls

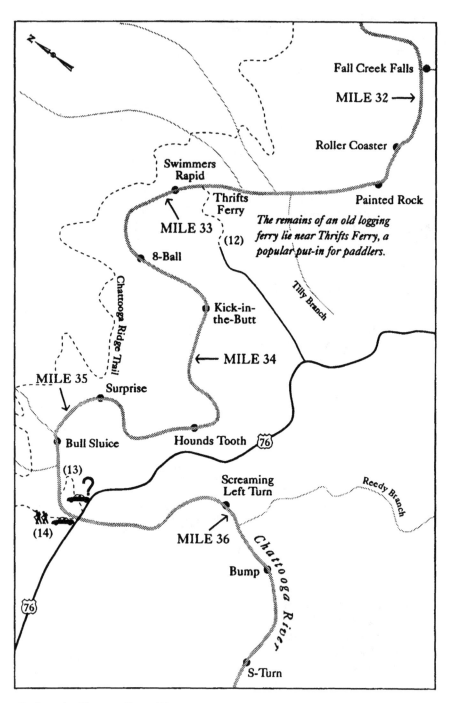

N

Fall Creek Falls

MILE 32 →

Roller Coaster

Painted Rock

Swimmers
Rapid

Thrifts
Ferry

MILE 33

(12)

*The remains of an old logging
ferry lie near Thrifts Ferry, a
popular put-in for paddlers.*

8-Ball

Tilly Branch

Kick-in-
the-Butt

MILE 34 ←

Chattooga Ridge Trail

MILE 35

Surprise

Bull Sluice

Hounds Tooth

76

(13)

?

(14)

Screaming
Left Turn

Reedy Branch

MILE 36 ↗

Bump

Chattooga River

76

S-Turn

Guide to the Chattooga River–58

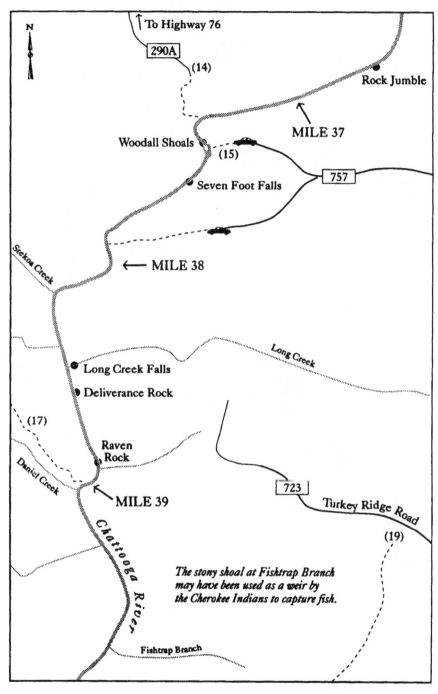

N

↑ To Highway 76

290A

(14)

Rock Jumble

MILE 37

Woodall Shoals

(15)

Seven Foot Falls

757

Stekoa Creek

← MILE 38

Long Creek

Long Creek Falls

Deliverance Rock

(17)

Raven Rock

Daniel Creek

MILE 39

723

Turkey Ridge Road

(19)

*The stony shoal at Fishtrap Branch
may have been used as a weir by
the Cherokee Indians to capture fish.*

Chattooga River

Fishtrap Branch

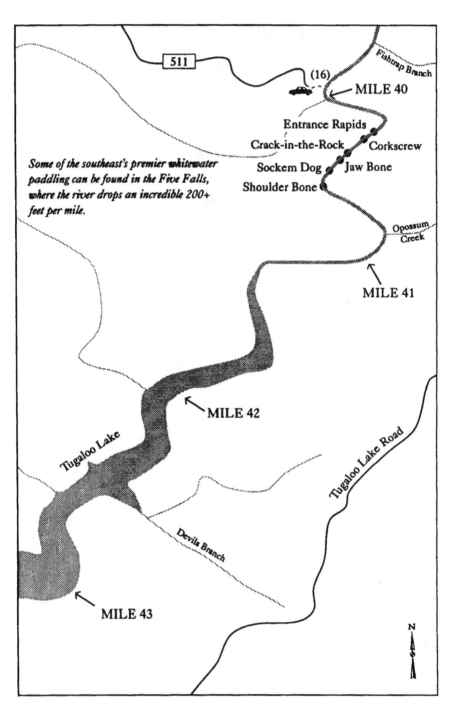

511

(16)

MILE 40

Fishtrap Branch

Entrance Rapids

Crack-in-the-Rock   Corkscrew

Sockem Dog   Jaw Bone

Shoulder Bone

Some of the southeast's premier whitewater paddling can be found in the Five Falls, where the river drops an incredible 200+ feet per mile.

Opossum Creek

MILE 41

MILE 42

Tugaloo Lake

Tugaloo Lake Road

Devils Branch

MILE 43

N

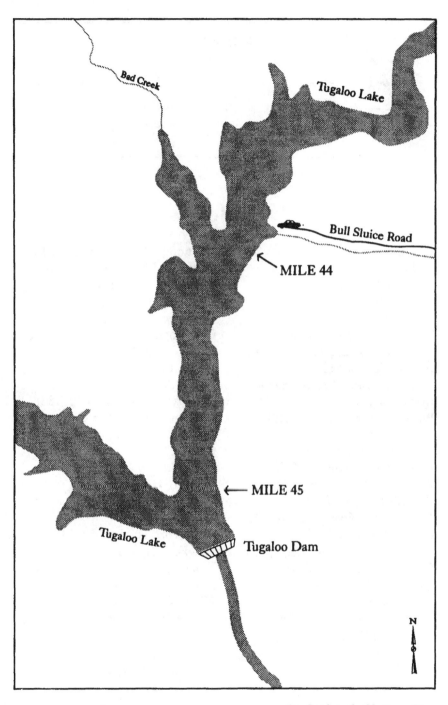

Bad Creek

Tugaloo Lake

Bull Sluice Road

← MILE 44

← MILE 45

Tugaloo Lake

Tugaloo Dam

N

Map Key

🚗	Parking	- - - - - -	Trail	
🚶	Trailhead	**?**	Information Station	
——	Paved Road	~~~~~~	River or Tributary	
——	Unpaved Road	☀	Mountain	

Index

Avifauna, 36-38
Bad Creek Trail, 46
Bartram, John, 34
Bartram National Recreation
    Trail, 44
Bartram Trail Association, 44
Bartram, William, 20, 29, 34, 44
Birds of the Carolinas, 38
Birds of the Blue Ridge Mountains, 38
Black bear, 35
Black Diamond Railroad, 23
Blue Ridge Railroad, 23
Blue Ridge Parkway, 9
Blue Ridge Mountains, 9-10, 17
Bull Sluice Portage Trail, 45
Burrel's Ford, 17, 22, 43
Burrel's Ford Camping Area, 42
Camp Creek Trail, 46
Cashiers, North Carolina, 6, 8, 40
Chattooga Ridge Trail, 45
Chattooga River, see
    Geology, 9-11
    Human History, 12-29
    Plant Life, 29-34
    Recreation, 41-49
    Weather, 11-12
    Wildlife, 34-41

Chattooga River Loop Trail, 43
Chattooga River Sourcebook, 4-5
Chattooga River Trail, 43
Chattooga River Trail, 46
Chattooga Town, 15-16, 17
Chattooga Watershed, 7, 8, 20, 39
Cherokee Indians, 13-17
    Myths, 14
    Settlements, 15-17
Cherokee Removal Act of 1838, 17
Civilian Conservation Corps, 25-26
Cleveland, Benjamin, 19
Cofitachiqui, 17
Commisioner's Rock, 22
De Soto, Hernando, 17-18
Dick' Creek Trail, 45
Earl's Ford, 43
Earl's Ford Portage Trail, 44
East Fork Trail, 47
Ellicot, Andrew, 21
Ellicot Rock, 21-22, 46
Ellicot Rock Trail, 46
Ellicott Rock Wilderness Area, 42,
    45, 46-47, 49
English, 14, 18-19
Fall Creek Portage Trail, 44
Fish, 39-41

Fish Hatchery Trail, 46
Fishing, 49
Five falls, 48-49
Foothills National Recreation
    Trail, 44
Foothills Trail Conference, 44
Fort Prince George, 34
*Georgia Conservancy's Guide to the
    North Georgia Mountains,* 43
Great Lakes Iroquoi, 14
Great Smoky Mountains National
    Park, 9
Hawks, 36, 37-38
Highlands, North Carolina, 8, 40
Hiking and camping, 42-43
Indian summer, 12
King Creek Falls Trail, 44
King George II, 21
Lake Jocassee, 21, 36
Lake Tugaloo, 9, 47, 49
Lake Yonah, 10
Leopold, Aldo, 5
Lick Log Trail, 45
Michaux, Andre, 20-21
Minerals, 10-11
Monroe House, 22
Mooney, James, 14-15
Nantahala Outdoor Center, 48
National Wild and Scenic River
    System, 4, 5, 6, 27-28
Native Americans, 12-21
Norwood's Station, 19
Oc mee Bells, 21, 32
Oconee Station, 19, 20
Opossum Creek Trail, 46
Orphan Strip, 21
Osprey, 37-38
Outfitters, 48
Owls, 36, 37

Paleo-Indians, 13
Peregrine falcons, 38
Raven Rock Trail, 46
Reptiles and Amphibians, 38-39
Ridley, Oliver, 24
Sandy Ford Portage Trail, 44
Savannah River, 10, 16, 29
Schroedl, Gerald, 16
Sloan Bridge Trail, 46
Soft Paths, 41
Southeastern Blue Ridge
    Escarpment, 7-9
Southeastern Expeditions, 48
Southern Appalachian
    Ecosystem, 9
Splash dams, 24
Spoon Auger Falls Trail, 44
Stumphouse tunnel, 23
Sutton Hole Trail, 45
Tallulah River, 14
Thrift's Ferry Trail, 45
Tilly Branch Trail, 45
Trails, 47
Travels of William Bartram, 20, 29
Trout, 40-41
Tugaloo River, 19, 43
Walhalla Fish Hatchery, 49
Warblers, 36, 37, 38
Weeks Law of 1911, 24
Where Have all the Birds Gone, 38
White-tailed deer, 34-35
Whitesides Mountain, 6, 8
Whitewater rafting, 47
Wild turkey, 37
Wildwater, Ltd., 48
Wolves, 34
Woodall Shoals Portage, 45
Woodpeckers, 36

Author's Acknowledgements

Without the patience and compassion of my friend and editor at Menasha Ridge Press, Budd Zehmer, I might have thrown this Chattooga manuscript in the same river on several different occasions. Thank you, Budd, for all the time you spent with my manuscript and with me on the telephone working through so many different narrow straits. Another friend of mine at Menasha, Mike Jones, helped see this book through from start to finish, and probably did more in my defense on certain points than I even know about.

I'd like to thank all three of the Chattooga River outfitters for funding the project. All proceeds from the sale of the book will go into a fund to promote educational programs about the river. That's a good idea.

My friend Tina Harrison gave me the run of the Whetstone office and computer, thereby making my work a whole lot easier than it might have been otherwise.

Jody Tinsley helped me with geology, both in this effort and previously, with the original Chattooga Sourcebook. It is my priviledge and a great pleasure to get to work with Jody on this river and to talk, at length, about rocks and trees and bugs and such.

Dr. Gerald Schroedl of the University of Tennessee was very generous with his time; his archaeological investigations at Chattooga Town have helped us all see deeper into the mystery of this place.

Robert Katz kindly reviewed my sections on avifauna, as did Perry Shatley of the US Forest Service.

Chaz Zartman, a botonist at Western Carolina University, helped me with wildflowers.

Dennis Chastain provided much invaluable information on trout in this watershed, and reviewed my writings on the same.

Mr. Hurley Badders at the Pendleton Historical Society sent me maps which helped me understand early settlement patterns on the Chattooga.

I thank everyone who helped in this project; there were many who gave me support and encouragement throughout.

Not least, I would like to thank the river people, past and present, from those first few who helped get it protected to all who seek to protect it now. With a tip of the hat to Forest B. Green.

CPSIA information can be obtained
at www.ICGtesting.com
Printed in the USA
JSHW042206310821
18290JS00002B/5